# UNDERSTANDING
# STRESS
# BREAKDOWN

To Nicola
God love you
Bill Wilkie

# UNDERSTANDING STRESS BREAKDOWN

**Dr William Wilkie**

Newleaf

Newleaf
an imprint of
Gill & Macmillan Ltd
Goldenbridge
Dublin 8
with associated companies throughout the world
www.gillmacmillan.ie

First published by Newleaf 1999
Copyright © 1995 William Wilkie

Printed in Malaysia

0 7171 2919 5

A catalogue record is available for this book from
the British Library.

5  4  3  2  1

# Contents

**INTRODUCTION**

Most of us know that too many worries can strain relationships with workmates, harm our health and destroy marriages. What we may not realize is how much damage is caused by our failure to understand the behavior of overstressed people. This book was written to explain why people behave the way they do under excessive stress.

This new edition (the third) is in response to many requests from people participating in seminars given by the author, for the inclusion of material on bullying and male/female differences covered in the seminars but not in the book. The book's basic message, however, is unchanged: that the mechanism of stress breakdown can be best understood in three easily identifiable stages, each stage produced by a different process. And when we understand these processes clearly, we are in a position to prevent stress breakdown by making some simple, clear choices.

Unfortunately for readers the literature on stress has been anything but clear. The confusion began with writers differing widely on what stress is, and continued with correspondingly differing advice. The word stress used to refer to a burden, load or emphasis. Engineers speak of stresses on structures or an orator might stress a point in a speech. However, in recent years, writers in this area have increasingly misused the word *stress* as synonymous with distress. People have been described therefore as suffering stress or experiencing stress. Not unexpectedly, readers have been mystified by the use of the one word *stress* to refer to both a cause of nervous system overload and the result of nervous system overload.

The confusion is compounded when prominent health professionals such as the late Dr Ainslie Meares define stress as a state of disequilibrium. In the beginning of his last book *Life Without Stress,* Ainslie Meares says, "As I see it, stress is the disharmony of brain function that arises when our brain is unable to integrate all the information it receives. Looked at in a more homely way, stress is the disparity between the adverse circumstances of our life and our ability to cope with them."

Is stress the load, the reaction, or the disparity? We cannot expect the physicists, engineers and orators to begin using a different word for burden, load or emphasis, to rescue us from our confusion. In this book, stress is used in its original meaning. The terms **stress breakdown** and **stress reaction** refer to a significant impairment of function, resulting from excessive load on the nervous system.

The first two editions of this book have been widely read, and the author has been gratified by comments suggesting that it has proved its worth in teaching ordinary readers to recognize the symptoms of stress breakdown and to react appropriately. A considerable number of people have claimed the book saved their marriage.

As well as clearing up some of the confusion

about stress, it is hoped this edition will also contribute to the general debate about a number of important issues. The victimization of ordinary people in schoolyards, bedrooms and workplaces, and the massive cost of doing nothing about it, is of increasing public concern. Another worrying problem is the number of people dependent on drugs needlessly prescribed for stress symptoms. A third area of concern is the difficulty wives and husbands have in trying to comprehend the basic differences between them. In recent years, people have been reluctant to talk about male/female differences for fear of being regarded as being prejudiced or "chauvinistic." Yet another issue raised by this book is our ignorance of the needs of mothers of newborn infants.

I am very grateful for the support and encouragement of the most important people in my life: Susanne, Lisa and Michael. It was my wife Susanne who suggested I should write this book in the first place, and her considerable literary skills have helped to make it readable.

**William Wilkie**

# CHAPTER ONE
## The Signs of Stress Breakdown

The first sign you are beginning to break down from too much stress is that you suddenly experience free-floating anxiety.

Free-floating anxiety is a vague, urgent feeling of unease or dread.

At the same time you may feel tense and easily startled. You may also experience symptoms in various parts of your body, caused by the body's being prepared to run away or fight.

If you stay in the stressful situation, using your willpower and your energy reserves to keep going, you may also experience, as well as anxiety, one or both of the two symptoms of the second stage of stress breakdown:

• Loss of the ability to control your emotions. You may flare up suddenly into anger, tears or laughter.

• Loss of the ability to motivate yourself. You will be unable to force yourself to get back to work. Your "get up and go" will seem to have got up and gone.

If you still cannot find relief from the stressful

situation, you may then experience the symptoms of the third stage of stress breakdown:

• You may suddenly find many forms of stimulation quite disagreeable, and you will tend to withdraw emotionally and avoid sensory stimulation. You may find noise, bright lights, people touching you, tight clothing and music, intolerable.

• You may suddenly lose the ability to *not react* to things you have previously put up with for years. You may become intolerant of faults and failings in others and in yourself.

• You may appear to others to have undergone a personality change. Important responsibilities will now seem to be ignored while you continue to react normally to unimportant matters.

If you try to continue coping with stress that has caused you to experience these three different groups of stress symptoms, you may become seriously ill, unable to carry out your normal duties and functions. This illness may take the form of a mental illness, an emotional illness, or a physical illness.

In any case, you will also experience major communication difficulties with your workmates and loved ones. You may even come to believe—quite wrongly—that your marriage or love relationship has broken down.

Don't panic! As you learn what causes these stress symptoms, you will find ways of avoiding stress-caused illness and stress-caused relationship breakdown.

Here is a poem to help you remember the three main groups of symptoms we find in stress breakdown:

*Is the stress of modern living breaking up your home?*
*You might recognize it in this little poem.*

*Talk about stress breakdown: the very first sign*
*Is feeling tense and nervy most of the time.*

*And if you don't work out what's getting you uptight*
*And you just go on willpower, thinking you'll be all right,*

*Two things can happen when your battery runs down:*
*You can find yourself just sitting around—*
*Can't get started—*
*Or flying off the handle, bursting into tears*
*Getting more emotional than you've been in years.*

*The family might recognize you're going off your head*
*And lovingly suggest you spend the day in bed.*

*There are three stages in stress breakdown,*
*I've mentioned one and two,*
*And I won't be surprised at all,*
*If what I said, you already knew.*
*But here's the situation that really worries me:*
*Only just a very few can recognize stage three.*

*Stage three symptoms can't be underestimated,*
*For many people wrongly think love's just*
*    deteriorated.*

*Suddenly you can't stand noise or any*
*    stimulation*
*You just want to get away from the whole*
*    situation.*

*All your loved one's faults and failings you never*
*    criticize,*
*Suddenly you just can't stand—they're*
*    intolerable in your eyes.*

*And your reaction pattern changes*
*Big problems you don't see*
*While unimportant details you treat attentively.*

*When all these things are happening,*
*That we don't comprehend,*
*Love relationships are weakened,*
*On which family life depends.*

# CHAPTER TWO
## The Warning Signal

Everyone breaks down under stress. Every one of us has a breaking point beyond which we all experience the symptoms of stress breakdown. If we draw a graph of mental performance in relation to arousal level or stress level, the result is a curve like an upside down letter "U". As stress or arousal level increases, we find performance increases to a peak, and beyond that peak, further arousal or stress just results in a falling-off of performance. This inverted U curve is also known as the Yerkes-Dodson Law, and has been known to psychologists for many years.

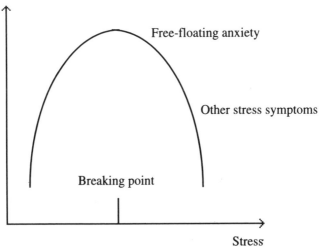

Performance

Free-floating anxiety

Other stress symptoms

Breaking point

Stress

If we draw graphs for different personalities, we find that quiet sensitive introverted people tend to break down at a lesser level of stress than do the rowdy, stimulus-seeking extraverts. However, the graph also reveals that introverts work more efficiently at lower levels of arousal. These are the self-supervising people who work best when they are left alone to get on with the job. Extraverts, on the other hand, usually need constant encouragement and supervision for full efficiency.

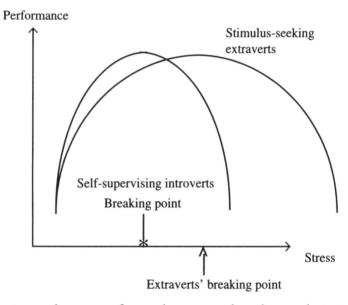

It might seem from these graphs above that it would not be difficult to choose personnel for high stress jobs—just choose stimulus-seeking extraverts. However, such attempts at selecting people for high stress jobs on the basis of personality type usually fail. The main reason is that many high stress jobs in military, police, and emergency services require sensitive, perceptive people who can work alone without supervision. And the people who do these jobs best often turn out to be the sensitive introverts with a lower threshold for stress breakdown.

It is my experience that children regularly victimized at school are usually self-supervising introverts and the bullies are usually stimulus-seeking extraverts. The bullies enjoy the sport and the feeling of power from imposing sufficient stress on their sensitive introverted victims to cause stress breakdown symptoms.

## Free-floating anxiety

If we are asking the brain to handle more information than it can comfortably process, or carry out some task that is too difficult, a warning signal is fired off, adrenalin is released into the bloodstream and we will experience a feeling of unease or dread plus the symptoms of body arousal for fight or flight. This feeling is called *free-floating anxiety*.

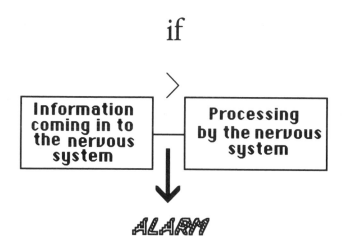

if

| Information coming in to the nervous system | Processing by the nervous system |

ALARM

*A feeling of vague but urgent
unease or dread
and
The body is prepared to run
away or fight*

17

It is called "free floating" because it doesn't seem to be attached to anything unlike, for example, a fear of spiders, where a feeling of anxiety is attached to the possibility of encountering spiders. With free-floating anxiety, you feel worried or anxious or tense but you don't know why. Psychiatrists usually refer to free-floating anxiety simply as anxiety, and anxiety attached to specific objects or situations as phobic or situational anxiety.

**Anxiety is no more or no less than an alarm signal triggered by the brain when it is having difficulty processing the information being presented to it.**

When you experience the symptoms of anxiety (vague but urgent unease or dread plus body tension symptoms), it is not difficult to work out why, in a large number of cases.

**You can suddenly experience free-floating anxiety if you are:**

- **Trying to do too many things at once, or** ⸜
- **Trying to do something too difficult, like:**
  Waiting, when you don't know how long.
  Having to go along with people changing their minds frequently.
  A no-win situation—whatever decision you make, whatever alternative you choose, you are going to suffer for it.

**Or you might experience free-floating anxiety under a normal workload if the brain's processing capacity has been impaired by:**

⸜ Insufficient **sleep**

Poor **nutrition**—low blood glucose, vitamin deficiency
**Illness** and hormone deficiency states
**Alcohol** and sedative drug withdrawal
Excessive **stimulants** such as tea and coffee

Anxiety is a symptom that everyone experiences. Some people, however, feel anxious so often that their quality of life is severely impaired, and their condition comes to be looked upon as an illness, such as *generalized anxiety disorder.* Sometimes anxiety occurs only in a certain situation where a person has broken down under stress. This may be called a *traumatic stress disorder.* Sometimes people become so worried about the possibility of feeling anxious, that whenever they feel anxious their fear rapidly escalates into what we call *panic disorder.*

There are many examples of human distress involving the feeling of anxiety. However, whatever the pattern, the basic cause of the anxiety can always be found by examining what is happening in the nervous system at that exact moment. We should remember that anxiety is no more and no less than an alarm signal that says the brain cannot comfortably process the incoming information at that time.

At times, the basic processing difficulty in a case of unexplained anxiety can be difficult to discern. Sometimes the cause will be found in subconscious mental conflict: the person has actually forgotten an underlying no-win conflict because it is too difficult or painful to face. It takes highly trained experts to uncover the causes of anxiety in these cases. However, in the majority of cases, it is not difficult for

19

untrained people to work out why they have begun to experience free-floating anxiety, simply by remembering the situations the brain finds difficult to deal with, and the usual reasons for a reduction in the brain's processing capacity.

## The body symptoms of anxiety

Anxiety does two things: it warns us something is wrong somewhere, and it prepares us to run as fast as we can, or fight, if necessary. Why run or fight? Because although we live in a space-age world we still have bodies designed to react to primeval dangers. Our nervous systems are wired up to expect that a threat to our lives will be something with fangs. When instead the threat to our existence is posed by rising interest rates and falling commodity prices, it is not really appropriate to have our bodies prepared for fight or flight. Running away is not going to reduce the threat to our existence. In this high tech world, anxiety which might help us survive a stone-age threat, just makes us feel physically uncomfortable.

However, running does in fact relieve some of the symptoms of anxiety, using up the adrenalin, the muscle tension and the extra blood glucose. Strenuous physical exercise helps reduce body symptoms of anxiety.

As you might imagine, preparing the body for possible urgent physical action involves a number of changes to different systems in the body. To remember what these changes are and what symptoms we might expect, all we need to do is picture what body changes would help us run faster or fight better.

- The state of tension of the muscle fibers increases, making them contract more efficiently and quickly.

- Blood supply is redirected to decrease blood flow to skin, internal digestive organs and kidneys, and to increase the blood flow to brain, heart, and muscles.

- The pulse rate increases, pushing nutrients faster around the body, providing more oxygen and carrying away more carbon dioxide. The rate of breathing increases.

- The nervous system's automatic reflexes are sharpened, the person becomes vigilant and is able to react faster.

- Glycogen in the liver breaks down into glucose, increasing the available nutrient supply to heart, brain, and muscle.

We can therefore expect the symptoms of anxiety to fall into groups, associated with these body changes in preparation for fight or flight.

**Increased muscle tension**

Symptoms are usually of soreness, stiffness, pain, fatigue and increased twitching. The muscle groups worst affected by anxiety are those that cannot rest easily. The chest muscles cannot rest because they need to keep us breathing to stay alive. The lower back muscles can only rest when we are lying down. Likewise the muscles of the neck and upper shoulders which hold the head up straight all day. Headaches, backaches and pains in the chest are

21

common physical symptoms of anxiety. As well, the increased tension of both agonist and antagonist muscle groups causes tremor, or shakes, seen most easily in the hands.

It is thought also that prolonged muscular contractions occurring in anxiety states may interfere with the easy pumping of blood through the tightened muscles. The result is that the contracted muscles become relatively starved of oxygen and this results in more acid waste products than usual. These acid products may contribute to muscle soreness and stiffness.

## Heightened reflexes and hypervigilance

The sharpening of nervous system reflexes, together with the increased vigilance, tend to interfere with the ability to sleep. Usually this means having difficulty getting off to sleep, but sometimes it will cause the person to wake up more readily during the night.

## The changes in blood supply and function of the internal organs

Anxiety symptoms over a prolonged period can cause a number of problems in the abdominal organs. The preparation for fight or flight is the function of the *sympathetic nervous system*—one of the automatic regulatory systems overseeing all the necessary processes going on in your body at this moment. Most organs have *sympathetic* and *parasympathetic* fibers, which oppose each other. Just as the interaction between a motor car's accelerator and brake controls the speed of the car, the interaction between sympathetic and parasympathetic activity controls the function of many organ systems in the body. Prolonged anxiety can change this happy equilibrium and cause spasm in hollow organs like the large bowel and bladder, and dyspepsia from disordered contractions of the stomach.

**Effects on heart and circulation**

People who are anxious usually appear pale in the face. This is a sign of the shutting down of blood-flow through the skin, and this diversion of blood-flow plus some sweating will make the hands feel cold and clammy. The anxious person often notices a rapid heart rate and may also experience flutters and palpitations due to occasional irregular heart beats. These abnormal beats result from an increased irritability of the heart caused by activation of the sympathetic nervous system fibers.

Fainting can also occur in long-standing anxiety, and is caused by the parasympathetic nervous system fibers suddenly slowing the heart rate as the opposing sympathetic (accelerator) fibers fatigue and stop firing when an already anxious person is faced with an acute crisis.

## When you suddenly feel anxious

You suddenly experience a vague urgent feeling of unease or dread. It is as though you are worried about something but you don't know what it is. Then you notice you're a little shaky, your palms are sweaty, you feel a deep gnawing pit in your stomach, your legs feel rubbery, your back feels stiff. You're sighing, breathing more rapidly. Your chest feels heavy, as though it's difficult to get a satisfying breath. Your heart skips a beat. You take your pulse, it's 120 beats a minute. Someone says you look pale. You feel terrible.

23

This is free-floating anxiety. It is only an alarm signal telling you that your brain is not able to carry out what you are asking it to do right now.

Is this stress breakdown? Are you trying to do too many things at once? If you are a housewife and mother, lover, tutor, transport driver, sports coach, first aid expert, motivational consultant and short-order cook, the answer could be yes! If you are a man trying to do two things at once, the answer could also be yes!

The sad truth is that many men don't seem to be able to do more than one thing at a time. For many years I have been approached by worried women concerned their husbands could be showing early signs of Alzheimer's Disease. "Doctor, I think my husband's got brain damage. If we're doing the dishes, and I ask him a question about politics, he'll have to stop in the middle of drying a plate, answer the question, and then go back to drying the plate. Is this serious, doctor?" These women are relieved but a little incredulous when I tell them that most men are like this.

If you are anxious and you are not doing too many things at once, is what you are trying to do, too difficult? There are three situations the human brain has great difficulty with:

- **Waiting.** Waiting for something to happen, when you don't know how long it will be, is something that always makes us anxious. You hear the man in the upstairs apartment take off one shoe and drop it on the floor. You wait for the other shoe to drop. It doesn't! After waiting three minutes you want to ring him up and accuse him of playing mind games. Some people who have trained themselves to tolerate waiting can go into a self-induced hypnotic trance. Other people feel they must occupy themselves with some task like reading. When we cannot entertain ourselves enough or the waiting is too long, human beings become very distressed. Our society uses prolonged waiting as a punishment—imprisonment.

- **Having to adapt to rapidly changing circumstances.** People become anxious when they have to adapt to situations which continually reverse themselves. People keep changing the place where you are supposed to pick them up in heavy traffic. You are the receptionist having to explain to the public why what was wrong last week is now preferred policy, and the word comes down that they have changed it all back again. Change is often so bothersome to people that we say things like "the devil you know is better than the devil you don't know." Sometimes we would rather put up with an inconvenience we are used to than take a risk on something unknown that may or may not be better.

- **Being in a no-win situation.** When we are forced to choose between two equally unacceptable alternatives, and we cannot get out of having to do this, we will experience anxiety. The great Russian physiologist Ivan Pavlov did some very elegant research on experimental stress breakdown in his laboratory using dogs as subjects. A dog was trained to respond to the sight of a circle on a card with a particular action, in order to be fed. He was also trained not to respond to the sight of an ellipse on a card, or else he would not be fed. Then they asked the hungry dog to respond to cards on which the axes of the ellipse were changed so that the dog found it hard to tell if the imprint on the card was a fat ellipse or a lumpy circle. He knew if he made the wrong response he would not be fed. Suddenly, he refused to cooperate, bit the experimenter and began barking furiously. The dog experienced stress breakdown.

There are many jobs in which a day's work is a series of no-win situations: police work, for example. When a police officer charges somebody with an offense someone may accuse him of victimization. If he fails to charge that person, someone else may accuse him of corruption. Similarly, the disciplinary role of parent or teacher provides an endless stream of no-win situations.

## Have I had enough sleep?

Perhaps your anxiety is not caused by excessive load. Have you had enough sleep? If you use an alarm clock to wake you in the morning, you probably are not getting enough sleep. When you are getting sufficient sleep, you will wake up before the alarm goes off.

Although every person knows from experience how important it is to get sufficient sleep, science still hasn't fully explained what sleep does. We know it is necessary to keep the brain from becoming overstimulated, because the inhibitory neurotransmitters are only generated during sleep. We know that a certain level and amount of deep sleep is necessary for restoration and repair of muscles and ligaments. Deep sleep is also essential in keeping up normal numbers of the body's white blood cells, which protect us against invaders and destroy cancer cells. We know also that dreaming sleep is useful in helping us deal with traumatic situations. But in spite of all we already know, research on sleep is still discovering new facts and posing new questions.

I am personally content to accept William Shakespeare's description of sleep, from *Macbeth* Act II:

*Sleep that knits up the ravelled sleeve of care,*
*The death of each day's life, sore labour's bath,*
*Balm of hurt minds, great nature's second course,*
*Chief nourisher in life's feast-*

Shakespeare says it all in describing the recuperative function of sleep and its relationship to stress breakdown.

### What is the state of my nutrition? In particular, my blood glucose.

While other body organs can use nutrients other than glucose as fuel the brain cannot. So when the level of glucose in the blood drops, brain function is impaired and an anxiety reaction occurs immediately. Adrenalin released into the bloodstream causes glycogen in the liver to break down into glucose, fairly rapidly restoring the blood glucose level to normal. This glycogen-breakdown mechanism takes about 20–30 minutes.

Hypoglycemia (low blood glucose) is a common occurrence in the lives of diabetic patients treated with insulin. The sudden onset of anxiety is a useful warning of hypoglycemia, giving the patient time to take some extra sugar. Hypoglycemia can occur also in other conditions, notably functional hypoglycemia. The patient with this disorder is usually either too fat or too thin, and has usually been consuming too much refined carbohydrate. In this disorder the fasting blood glucose level will be normal, but at a particular interval following a carbohydrate meal, the blood glucose drops below the fasting level. At that time, the nervous system will become inefficient and trigger off an anxiety reaction.

### Pills or alcohol wearing off?

Withdrawal of sedative drugs, such as alcohol and the benzodiazepine drugs such as diazepam (Valium), oxazepam (Serepax), lorazepam (Ativan), bromazepam (Lexotan), temazepam (Normison) and nitrazepam (Mogadon), can produce an agitation indistinguishable from anxiety. Most people have experienced hangovers from drinking alcohol, but they may not realize that sedative drugs prescribed for anxiety will leave a vague agitation when the sedation wears off. Thus, a person may be suffering from feelings of anxiety due simply to withdrawal of the sedative action of a drug, leaving the agitation.

### Too much tea, coffee or cola drinks?

Another common cause of feeling agitated is the consumption of excessive amounts of tea, coffee, and cola drinks containing caffeine. The caffeine and other drugs in these drinks cause stimulation by release of noradrenaline in the body. Excessive amounts of stimulants can produce a state indistinguishable from severe anxiety.

## Do I need to see a doctor?

When a person is developing a physical illness, the brain's processing abilities may be impaired and stress breakdown may occur at lower levels of stress than otherwise would be tolerated. The illness need not be a condition primarily affecting brain function, such as meningitis or encephalitis; many different disorders may cause relative failure of the brain's processing capacity. For example, fever from any cause can so disturb brain function as to produce delirium at times. When the onset of such an illness is gradual, the first sign of being ill may well be the sudden onset of anxiety symptoms in response to a normal workload.

We often find a number of factors combining to reduce the brain's processing capacity. Many of us are too fat and too unfit; we smoke, we drink alcohol and abuse stimulant drugs, such as caffeine; we eat the wrong foods at the wrong times; we have irregular sleeping hours, and often don't relax. And we often start a working day with our nervous systems so compromised we have little hope of avoiding some level of stress breakdown.

A poem to remind you of the common causes of anxiety:

*I'm feeling nervy, perhaps it's that I'm*
*Doing too many jobs at the one time,*
*Or do I need help for this problem of mine?*

*No, the work's not excessive. My processing's slow.*
*Have I had enough sleep? Is my blood glucose low?*
*Or is there something wrong, I should know?*
*Is the booze wearing off, or is it the pills?*
*Too much tea or coffee, I hope I'm not ill?*

*If my little poem gives you a clue,*
*Stop what you're doing for a minute or two,*
*And think without panicking what you should do.*
*You're feeling so dreadful but it's just an alarm,*
*Feeling anxious is awful, but does you no harm.*
*But if you're terribly scared you'll fall in a heap,*
*Here's a little advice I hope that you'll keep,*
*Get some rest from the stress*
*And a great deal more sleep.*

Because anxiety symptoms occur most often in overtired people trying to do too many things at once, the simple advice to stop what you are doing and have a sleep is quite often the only advice needed.

## Reducing anxiety without dealing with the basic cause

If you are experiencing anxiety symptoms you should work out what is causing it and do something about it. However, each day, the world spends a lot of money on ways of reducing anxiety without addressing basic causes.

The brain circuits that send out the warning signals of anxiety are very complex, highly developed networks in the brain surface. They are involved in fine judgment and in analyzing information coming in through the distance sense receptors—vision, hearing and smell. Nerve cells in this network are more sensitive to lack of oxygen, poisons and drugs, than are the more hardy cells doing basic brain tasks like controlling breathing and keeping the circulation going. This is why virtually anything that interferes with brain function will switch off the brain's fine judgment and anxiety warning circuits long before other brain functions are interfered with. Thus among the first signs of alcoholic intoxication we find an absence of anxiety and fear, along with defective judgment. Alcohol in higher doses will stop other brain functions, leading to death. We also find lack of judgment and loss of anxiety occurring as an initial symptom in many other toxic states, including nitrogen narcosis in diving accidents, and carbon monoxide poisoning from faulty automobile exhaust systems.

## Alcohol and sedative drugs

Alcohol stops anxiety symptoms so rapidly, sometimes in ten minutes or less, that it has become our society's favorite method of disabling the brain's fine judgment circuits. Unfortunately however, the brain's reaction to alcohol and sedative drugs produces a hangover effect, so that when the alcohol and drugs wear off the person feels worse than before.

As soon as the brain discovers its surface cells are being affected by alcohol or a prescribed sedative drug, it tries to wake the cells up by increasing the firing of the reticular activating system low down in the brain stem. After the drug effect wears off, the brain surface continues being stimulated because it takes quite a while for the lower brain centers to realize the brain is now in an overstimulated state. The overstimulated surface cells will be firing off anxiety signals for a period of time usually about four times the duration of the sedation. Thus the price to pay for sedation of two hours from alcohol is eight hours of agitation. A drug like diazepam providing say six hours of freedom from anxiety will produce 24 hours of low-grade anxiety.

## Diverting attention

Another way of switching off the anxiety warning cell systems is to give the brain something else to focus its attention on. Thus diverting the anxious person's attention to something far away from the origins of his fears may reduce anxiety, so long as his attention is distracted. Entertainment such as movies, plays and songs that help us escape for a time to another reality can provide temporary relief.

## Feeding, fighting and propagating the species

Likewise, in stressful situations we may involve the brain in some other activity that it prefers, so that it doesn't register anxiety as it usually does. It has been found, for example, that eating, fighting, and engaging in sexual activity will reduce anxiety in stressful situations. Clever therapists offer tea and biscuits to frightened clients. Airline staff schedule meals soon after takeoff, when they expect air travelers will be most anxious.

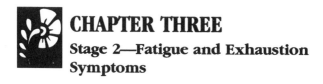

# CHAPTER THREE
## Stage 2—Fatigue and Exhaustion Symptoms

I have already said the first sign you are breaking down from trying to cope with too much stress is the warning signal of free-floating anxiety. If you cannot remove yourself from the stressful situation, you may be able to keep going for some time by calling on your inhibitory reserves and your willpower. But eventually these reserves will be depleted, and then two extra symptoms are added to the anxiety. These are the symptoms of:

- **Failure of emotional control.** You may suddenly burst into tears or laughter, or offer some irritable angry response.

- **Failure of the capacity for self-motivation.** You may find yourself just sitting around, unable to get started on all the jobs you have to do. But if someone else works with you, you can do the work. It's just that your own self-starter seems burnt out.

And you will need a rescuer to send you off to bed. These symptoms of stage two are caused by a rundown in your brain's neurotransmitter reserves, in particular your reserves of inhibitory neurotransmitters.

## Neurotransmitter Substances

When a brain cell is activated, it fires off electrically, and this firing-off releases a small amount of a chemical at the end of the nerve fiber. This chemical is called a neurotransmitter. The neurotransmitter substance in turn stimulates the next nerve cell to fire off. Thus the conduction of impulses in the brain is via an electrical-chemical process. Each nerve cell body may have the axon end plates of hundreds of other cells connected up to it. It usually takes a number of cells firing at once to provide the stimulus that makes the next nerve cell fire off, transmitting the message.

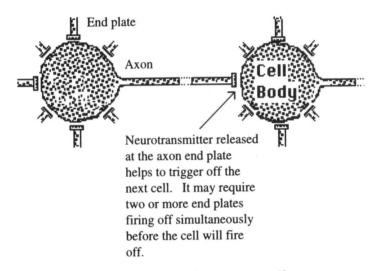

End plate

Axon

Cell Body

Neurotransmitter released at the axon end plate helps to trigger off the next cell. It may require two or more end plates firing off simultaneously before the cell will fire off.

A general reduction in the amount of neurotransmitter substance available for release will make the system less responsive. Thus by regulating these neurotransmitters, the brain can control its own sensitivity to incoming stimuli.

The most important neurotransmitter substances to be depleted under prolonged conditions of stress, are the inhibitory neurotransmitters. These substances released from nerve cell endings, instead of firing the next cell, actually inhibit the cell from firing. Certain networks of cells which inhibit the firing of other cells may form the brain's circuit breakers which switch off overloaded circuits. Other networks of inhibition help us control our tempers, our appetites, our bowels and our bladders; this is essential if we are to live in a give-and-take society.

Some of the most important of these inhibitory neurotransmitters can only be replaced by the brain when we are asleep. This is why depriving someone of sleep results in the brain becoming oversensitive and overstimulated. When inhibitory self-control neurotransmitters are not being generated, the brain may become dangerously overstimulated to the point where an epileptic seizure could occur.

It is not difficult to see how people depleted of essential nutrients in starvation and excessive dieting could quickly develop serious stress symptoms from a rundown of brain neurotransmitters. And people already in a weakened state, like the mothers of new-born babies, will rapidly develop serious stress breakdown symptoms because they don't have enough reserves. Teenagers getting little sleep, seeking emotional stimulation and eating junk food regularly, are similarly vulnerable to stress breakdown symptoms.

## Differentiating stage-two stress symptoms from depression and medical conditions

There are some symptoms of stage-two stress breakdown which can be mistaken for medical disorders. For example, tense, nervy people bursting into tears or losing their temper easily, while sitting around unable to get started on their work, might be wrongly diagnosed as suffering from endogenous depression or chronic fatigue syndrome.

The sleep disturbance of stress breakdown is the sleep disturbance of anxiety: difficulty in relaxing enough to go off to sleep. Once asleep, there is no difficulty staying asleep. With endogenous depression, on the other hand, the problem is staying asleep. The depressed person who will require medical treatment with antidepressants can usually get off to sleep quite readily, but may then wake early in the morning or sleep fitfully throughout the night. There is always a decrease in their time asleep, whereas in stress breakdown, once people get off to sleep, they will sleep a normal seven or eight hours. (Unless of course they are worried about a sick child and sleeping "with one eye open.") On the other hand, people suffering from chronic fatigue syndrome often complain of sleeping too much.

People suffering from depression usually feel worse in the mornings, their mood improving as the day wears on. The opposite is true for chronic fatigue syndrome and other medical conditions. After a sleep we have generated some energy and we feel better until the day's activities begin to tire us out. Physically ill people feel worse as the day wears on. If stress breakdown is the problem, the worst time of day will be when the particular stress is worst. If your stress problem is at work, you will feel better when you are home in the evenings. If your main problem is relationships at home, you will feel better at work.

**The symptom of fatigue**

Let us consider briefly some possible causes when the initial complaint is fatigue. Second-stage stress breakdown causes fatigue, but because the fatigue of stress breakdown is a brain tiredness rather than

36

a muscle tiredness, fatigue due to stress is often relieved by physical exercise. The fatigue associated with depression is always associated with a sleep problem, usually difficulty staying asleep. Tiredness and confusion lasting for half an hour at a time, late morning or late afternoon, is very likely to be caused by low blood glucose.

In chronic fatigue syndrome, people usually feel as if they are continually coming down with a virus. They feel weak and shivery and unable to think or concentrate properly. I usually identify four main causes of this chronic fatigue syndrome:

- Infections with viruses such as Epstein-Barr virus, enteroviruses, and Ross River virus. Bacterial infections like brucellosis, and parasitic infestations such as toxoplasmosis

- Food allergies

- Reactions to environmental chemicals such as insecticides and herbicides

- Overload of Candida albicans in the gastrointestinal tract

Because some of the symptoms seen in chronic fatigue syndrome and endogenous depression occur in stress breakdown, these three conditions are sometimes mistaken for one another.

### Sleeping "with one eye open"

The pattern of sleep disturbance is always an important clue to the type of depression that needs specific treatment with antidepressant drugs. In depression the problem is an inability to stay asleep, while in stress breakdown the difficulty is relaxing enough to get off to sleep. However, there is one notable exception to the usual pattern of sleep disturbance occurring in stress breakdown. This is when the stress involves some threat to the family. Overstressed people may sleep very lightly, waking frequently throughout the night, just as one might do in a tent in Africa somewhere, with leopards and other predators roaming around outside. I have found that women are particularly likely to respond to stress in this way, sleeping "with one eye open."

In these cases, an antidepressant drug of the tricyclic type is very useful. I often prescribe a small amount of doxepin, say 10 mg at night in these cases. Unlike the habit-forming sleeping tablets like nitrazepam (Mogadon) and temazepam (Normison), doxepin does not appear to have much potential for dependency.

## A note on depression

Endogenous depression, also called major depression or biological depression, is a mood disorder in which the person feels weak and tired, experiences broken sleep or early morning waking, feels worse at a particular time of day, especially in the mornings, and feels generally sad, sometimes enough to suicide. It is called endogenous because it is caused by some imbalance within the body's chemistry, rather than the result of a disappointment or loss. It is always important to recognize this condition because it is easily treated by appropriate medication, and also because if it is not treated medically, there is a significant risk of suicide.

So if a person you think is overstressed:

- is talking about suicide, and

- feels worse in the mornings, and   '

- is having difficulty staying asleep, or is waking early in the mornings, and

- has lost appetite and sexual drive,

you should get this person to a doctor as soon as possible.

## Aggression and violence in stage two

When people lose emotional control in a situation of high anxiety, violence may result. This is particularly so if the person is defending his or her "territory." One's "territory" might actually be one's own back-yard where someone is intruding uninvited. Or it might be a role, a job or a specific responsibility.

In stress breakdown, defensive aggression is apt to be sudden, unpredictable and violent, because of loss of emotional control. Violence is even more likely if the person under stress has been using alcohol, marijuana, or prescribed sedative drugs.

# CHAPTER FOUR
## Stress Symptoms and the Brain's Circuit Breakers

The reader may remember the attempted Soviet coup where Mikhail Gorbachev and his wife Raisa were held prisoner in their house in the Crimea. Raisa Gorbachev was reported to have suddenly lost the power to speak and the ability to use her right hand. When the crisis was over, she recovered these lost functions. This is an example of the operation of the brain's circuit breakers, networks of cells in the brain surface which switch off overloaded brain circuits, just as a circuit breaker in an electrical switchboard will switch off circuits in which too much current is flowing.

Raisa Gorbachev's diagnosis would have been a *conversion* state, where stress has been converted into a symptom. The sudden switching off can affect a range of brain functions, and cause various symptoms such as catatonia, dissociation and thought blocking. However, the brain's circuit breakers usually switch off overloaded brain circuits more slowly. And instead of the total absence of function as in Mrs Gorbachev's case, we usually see diminished responses in overloaded circuits. As we shall see, the brain's attempts to protect itself from overload causes the symptoms of third-stage stress breakdown.

## The law of strength of the nervous system

If I tap my patellar tendon just below the kneecap when my leg is flexed at the knee, the leg will extend.

41

This is the knee-jerk reflex. If I tap it harder, the reflex is more brisk and the response is stronger. Within limits, there is a simple law operating in the nervous system with regard to reflexes: a weak input stimulus will produce a weak response, and a stronger input stimulus will produce a stronger response.

Not only does this law of strength hold true for the reflexes in my body which are automatic and which I did not have to learn, but it also holds true for reflexes which I have learned during my life experiences. We have all experienced how learned skills become automatic after a while, as we become conditioned to respond in the same way, for instance driving a car, or riding a motorcycle. The clutch–gearshift coordination movements become so automatic that we don't even have to think about them after a while. These reflexes are called conditioned reflexes.

I once rode an Ariel 500cc motorcycle while I was studying first year medicine. After I had become reasonably adept at riding this motorcycle, I discovered something strange. Whenever I checked, while riding along, to see which gear the bike was in by touching the gear lever with my foot, the bike slowed down, unexpectedly and for no apparent reason. I then discovered that I had become so conditioned to cutting back the throttle with my right hand when I depressed the gear lever in changing gear, that simply touching the gear lever with my toe was automatically producing the wrist rotation which was causing the inadvertent throttling back. The two actions had been coordinated into a conditioned reflex which did not require me to be conscious of it.

The law of strength applies to these conditioned reflexes, as well as to the unlearned built-in reflexes such as the knee jerk reflex. That is, the conditioned response will be stronger if the input stimulus that triggers it is stronger. However, when the input is too strong the response will be diminished because of the operation of "circuit breaker" mechanisms. In exactly the same way as the circuit breakers in our domestic electrical circuits switch off the power if the current flowing in the circuit is too high, the brain can switch off overloaded circuits to protect itself from overload.

The brain's circuit breakers are cells near the brain surface, which release a neurotransmitter substance that actually inhibits the next cell from firing off. One such transmitter is gamma-amino-butyric acid or GABA.

This circuit breaker cell releases a different transmitter substance that inhibits the next cell from firing

Each nerve cell has a large number of end plates from other nerve cells impinging on the cell body. A number of these end plates firing at the same time will trigger the nerve cell to fire. But excessive firing will excite enough inhibitory cells to switch off the circuit.

So far we have seen that when an overstressed person begins to break down under stress:

The first symptom is a normal warning signal.
The next symptoms of stress breakdown are caused by fatigue.

The symptoms of the third stage are caused by the operation of the brain's circuit breakers.

## Symptoms of stage-three stress breakdown

We know someone is experiencing stage-three symptoms because of major changes in their behavior towards others close to them:

1. A relative intolerance of sensory stimulation.
2. A loss of the ability to ignore things which were previously tolerated.
3. Changed response patterns which superficially resemble a change of personality.

### Symptom 1—Avoidance of stimulation

Information comes in to the brain through sensory nerve fibers. Usually sensory nerves are activated by tiny sense organs or "receptors" which respond to certain sensations, and fire off the nerve. There are receptors for heat sensation, touch, position sense, balance, acceleration, cold, light, sound, taste and smell. As well, the muscles and the joints are supplied with stretch receptors which provide the information necessary for the body to know where its various parts are.

There does not seem to be a specific receptor for pain impulses. We experience pain from overstimulation of nerves which don't have specific sense receptors, and also whenever specific sensory receptors are overstimulated. Thus a too-loud noise, a too-cold stimulus, a too-hot stimulus, or a too-bright light, will all cause a feeling of pain.

In stress breakdown, the receiving brain cells are

so oversensitive that strong sensory stimulation becomes disagreeable, if not actually painful. Even stimulation which has previously been highly enjoyable, such as sexual stimulation, music, perfume, or exotic tastes, can become disagreeable in stress breakdown.

The discomfort caused by high levels of stimulation will cause the overstressed person to behave in such a way as to reduce incoming stimulation. This is the time, for example, when the overstressed person becomes seemingly suddenly interested in watering the lawn with a hand-held hose, with his back towards the house. The masking noise of the rushing water, the fact that people rarely insist on walking over wet grass to talk, and hosing being a solitary occupation, makes this a favorite activity of stressed people seeking to reduce sensory input. Pulling out weeds is another useful ploy. I remember once, in a period of overwhelming stress, just how interested I became in digging weeds out of the lawn with a dinner fork.

This symptom, avoidance of stimulation, is often misinterpreted by family members as sulking, self-centered arrogance, disdain or a lack of interest in the needs of others.

## Symptom 2—Loss of the ability to *not react*

There is a seeming double negative here. In third-stage stress breakdown it is suddenly impossible for you to *not react to* things you had previously trained yourself to *not react to.* In other words, you suddenly become unable to tolerate things you previously put up with.

The reason for this is that the nerve cells in the brain surface are being affected by the operation of the circuit breakers in complex ways, so that the overloaded conditioned reflexes are now in the paradoxical and ultraparadoxical phases of malfunction. These terms were invented by the great Russian scientist Ivan Pavlov. The neurophysiology of these malfunctioning conditioned reflexes is quite complex and need not concern us here. They are mentioned here to draw attention to the scientific studies which explain these stress reactions.

Until recently some police services were fairly intolerant of complaints of stress symptoms in officers. Police officers suffering from anxiety symptoms in stressful situations tended to be looked down on by their fellow officers and superiors, and were reluctant to report stress symptoms for fear of damaging their chances of promotion. Far too often, they would not report stress symptoms until they suddenly found themselves unable to not react to some provocation. It is a crazy and very dangerous situation; it makes no sense whatever to have as the first sign of stress breakdown the inability of an armed person to not react to provocation. It was somewhat like the situation with British aircrew in World War II, often selected by the RAF because they did not display anxiety symptoms readily under stress. Sometimes the first time a pilot displayed stress breakdown symptoms was when he deliberately flew his aircraft into the side of a hill.

Fortunately the situation is now improving, with more emergency services personnel adopting modern techniques of debriefing in response to major trauma and encouraging their staff to discuss their feelings openly.

## Symptom 3—Apparent change in personality and priorities

When the brain has to begin switching off overloaded circuits to protect itself, the law of strength which I mentioned before fails to operate. This is because strong stimuli cause switching off responses while weak stimuli do not. Therefore, the person with stage-three stress breakdown symptoms begins to respond inappropriately, failing to address major responsibilities while attending normally to unimportant matters. Not unexpectedly, this behavior quite mystifies his or her workmates and relatives.

Our personalities are often defined on the basis of our preoccupations. Obsessive people are preoccupied with lists and procedures, narcissistic people place a lot of emphasis on appearances, and so on. In third-stage stress breakdown, problems that bother us most may begin to evoke the least response, which is actually the opposite to the way we usually behave.

Because the behavior of a person exhibiting third-stage stress breakdown symptoms can be so out of character for that person, others find it difficult to describe their behavior adequately. Thus, members of the family or workmates of the overstressed person may sometimes resort to extreme psychiatric diagnoses or accusations of moral degeneration, because the overstressed person's behavior has become incomprehensible on the basis of their previous personality.

### Ignoring important issues, attending to trivia

As a result of being unable to respond to problems which would normally have top priority, the overstressed person might become apparently hopelessly disorganized, ignoring important decisions and busying themselves with trivia. The overstressed mother of the newborn baby may not be able to respond to the baby's cries appropriately.

An overstressed company general manager has to make a significant response to a real threat of industrial action from employees in a factory where a workmate has been killed accidentally. The union is concerned about safety procedures. The manager knows full well that a whole section of the factory is potentially unsafe, and needs rebuilding. However the board of directors has made it clear that the company is just surviving, and the general manager knows that the extra expenditure to fix up the factory floor will be the trigger for closing down the business and result in the loss of many jobs, including his own.

To make it more complex, the dead employee was clearly defying normal safety procedures, and the crisis might in fact be negotiable with the union. However, the general manager has just come out of hospital following an operation for suspected cancer, and his wife's father has just died. He is suffering from stress breakdown symptoms. The day he is to meet with the union representatives, he seems not to be able to arrange an agenda for the meeting, but instead is preoccupied with ordering more paperclips for his office.

The big problems appear not to be noticed by an overstressed person, appear not to "register" as important or top priority. Instead little problems receive an attention that is odd in the circumstances.

When this behavior is not recognized as due to stress breakdown, wrong assumptions may lead to totally inappropriate responses from others. The spouse of an overstressed person might complain that he or she seems to have changed priorities, or is deliberately ignoring the needs of the family. Misunderstanding this symptom can lead to people feeling emotionally hurt at the apparent about-face in attitude of the stressed person:

"He is so callous, doctor, and he just does not care any more. He thinks more of taking that dog for a walk than he does about helping me since I had my heart attack!"

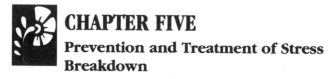

# CHAPTER FIVE
### Prevention and Treatment of Stress Breakdown

Regardless of other therapy, first-aid management of stress breakdown is:

Rest, relief from stress, and a lot more sleep. Remove the stress from the person or the person from the stress.

Drugs are often requested for the treatment of stress breakdown, even when the breakdown was clearly caused only by an unexpected and excessive stress. Why? I think people generally believe that mental illnesses controlled so well by psychiatrists' medication, such as schizophrenia, are caused by stress. Therefore they think the medication acts primarily to reduce the negative effects of stress. This is only partly true.

In practice, drugs have very little place in the correct treatment of stress breakdown, although they are often used, particularly the sedative drugs. Sedative drugs reduce fear and anxiety, and people under stress can temporarily feel a lot better taking alcohol, marijuana or a prescription sedative. However, the use of sedatives in stress breakdown is fraught with danger, for four main reasons:

- The sedated person tends to stay in the stressful situation.

- With the warning signal of anxiety switched off,

the overstressed person goes straight into second and third-stage symptoms.

- There is an increased tendency towards loss of control and violence.

- There is a real risk of drug dependence developing.

Of course, the best treatment for stress breakdown is prevention. But when stress breakdown has not been prevented, treatment usually proceeds in four steps:

1. accepting the fact of having broken down
2. treating the symptoms of stress breakdown
3. treating the causes of the stress breakdown
4. making sure it does not happen again

## Accepting the fact of having broken down

Many people feel devastated at the thought of having failed and having broken down under the stress of their responsibilities. Sometimes an overdeveloped sense of individual responsibility has caused them to stay in an impossible situation. Sometimes the very reason the task became too difficult was the excessively high standard they demanded from themselves.

How do we let people know it's OK to have experienced a stress breakdown? By explaining that everyone breaks down, given sufficient stress. The personal testimony of someone who has survived stress breakdown is very helpful. Some people feel cleansed by the experience. Now they know who their friends really are, and how marvellous are those simple things in their lives they previously took for granted.

## Treating the symptoms of stress breakdown

The first symptom of stress breakdown is anxiety, and we know that anxiety is simply an alarm signal. Therefore the appropriate treatment of anxiety is to remove whatever is triggering the alarm and the alarm will switch itself off. To do this, we begin by recalling the anxiety equation in Chapter 2.

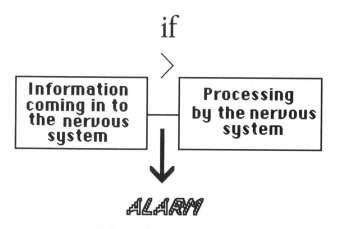

*A feeling of vague but urgent unease or dread*
*and*
*The body is prepared to run away or fight*

The imbalance between the task your brain is attempting and its processing capacity at that particular time is what is causing the alarm signal to fire. Therefore, when you experience anxiety, stop what you are doing. Immediately ask yourself two questions about what you have been doing:

1. "Am I trying to do too much?" *or*
2. "Is this too difficult for me?"

And then three questions to do with brain function:

3. "Have I had enough sleep?"
4. "What is the state of my nutrition—when and what did I eat last?"
5. "Is there something wrong?"

If you find a possible cause for the anxiety, for example trying to do something that's too difficult for you, you will know that when you restore the correct balance by getting help, the anxiety will stop. Likewise when the cause is low blood glucose, if you have something to eat or take glucose in a drink, the anxiety will stop.

However, some anxious people will be so worried about themselves they cannot concentrate on these objective questions. I have a few favorite devices to distract attention and produce a temporary reduction in anxiety:

Stop what you are doing and go to another room. Turn on the radio or TV and have something to eat. Have a nice warm shower and put on some comfortable clothes.

It may then be possible to relax enough to work out what caused the anxiety alarm signal in the first place.

**Am I trying to do too many things at once, or is what I am doing too difficult for me right now?**

It is often difficult for people to recognize when they are trying to do something too difficult for their nervous systems to process easily. Here are a few helpful questions:

- Are you waiting for something to happen?

- Are you attempting to change course, going back on your previously stated goals?

- Are you trying to protect others from suffering from the consequences of their own foolish behavior?

- Are you trying to extract guarantees from yourself about your future?

- Are you trying to deal with the loss of something by hardening your heart?

- Are you trying to stay angry at someone, or holding onto resentments?

- Are you setting out on a project, the prime purpose of which is to harm or upset someone else?

- Are you trying to deceive someone you love?

- Are you trying to convince others you are cleverer than they think you are?

- Are you trying to make a decision, the primary purpose of which is to protect yourself from being hurt emotionally?

- Are you trying to make a decision between two equal and opposite alternatives?

- Are you being forced into making a decision where the inevitable outcome—whatever your decision—is that someone will be hurt?

- Are you being harassed or criticized in a situation you cannot leave, such as your job?

## Check the diagnosis

Feeling states similar to free-floating anxiety can appear in various medical conditions. The very first step is therefore to check if what you are experiencing is free-floating anxiety.

1. Do you have a vague but urgent feeling of unease or dread, as though you are expecting something to go wrong, but you don't know what it is?
2. Do you feel "wound up," "up tight," "tense," jumpy, more easily startled, for example if the telephone rings unexpectedly?
3. Are you having some difficulty unwinding enough to get off to sleep easily at night?
4. Do you suffer from three or more of the following symptoms?
   (a) palpitations or rapid pulse rate
   (b) headaches
   (c) lower backache
   (d) feelings of heaviness in the chest
   (e) sharp pains coming from sore spots on the chest wall
   (f) discomfort in the upper part of the abdomen
   (g) increased frequency of passing urine
   (h) tremor or shakes of the hands
   (i) sweaty palms
   (j) stiffness of back and shoulder muscles
   (k) overbreathing and feelings of panic from time to time

If you answered "yes" to the first three questions, and "yes" to three or more of the symptoms in Question 4, then you have most probably been suffering from symptoms of anxiety. However, you could be suffering from a medical illness associated with:

Low blood-calcium levels
Excessive release of adrenalin
Low blood-glucose
Unexpected effects of drugs
Alcohol and sedative drug withdrawal
Temporal lobe epilepsy
High doses of asthma and sinus medications
Disorders of the thyroid gland
Premenstrual tension

Don't try to make these diagnoses yourself. See a doctor.

## Drugs for anxiety

In our society, the use and abuse of alcohol and prescription sedatives has become a major health problem. Sedative drugs prevent the anxiety response from occurring when the nervous system is overloaded. However, while they are relieving anxiety, they also interfere with brain function, affecting the ability to drive and work safely.

Which drugs are the sedatives? They are the drugs whose possible unwanted effects include habituation and dependence; the drugs that make you feel better no matter what the problem is, like alcohol, marijuana, chloral hydrate, barbiturates, and benzodiazepines. They reduce anxiety and fear, and produce a sort of brain numbness that many people find preferable to clear consciousness.

However, the lower centers of the brain don't like the way these drugs slow down the cells in the brain surface. So the reticular activating system responds by stimulating the cerebral cortex to wake it up, and as the drug effect begins to wear off, this stimulation is experienced as vague low-grade agitation. People feel more anxious after a sedative drug wears off than they would have if they hadn't taken the drug.

This withdrawal agitation usually leads to taking another dose. However, the agitation is additive and so multiple doses cause it to accumulate. We may then observe a strange paradox—repeated doses of a drug originally taken to produce a calming effect will ultimately produce a state of overexcitement and stimulation, as if you had injected the person with a stimulant drug like amphetamine. Multiple doses of alcohol or a prescription sedative can result in delirium tremens, with the brain in such an over-stimulated state that epileptic seizures can occur.

**Think carefully before using a sedative**

The risk of sedative dependence is so high when a person is being treated for stress breakdown symptoms that sedative drugs should only be given if the anxiety symptoms themselves have become the major cause for concern. Such is the case when the effects of anxiety on the heart are life-threatening, for example. Another instance might be when anxiety symptoms prevent a person from leaving the house. However, I believe that in the majority of cases of anxiety symptoms caused by stress overload, the use of sedative drugs cannot be justified.

**The use of beta-blocking drugs**

There may be some justification, however, for using beta-blocking drugs. These drugs are used by physicians to oppose the effects of adrenalin on the body, and are used to treat such conditions as high blood pressure, rapid and irregular heart rate and hyperthyroidism. They have also been found useful for treating body symptoms of anxiety.

These drugs are unlike sedatives in that they do not prevent the warning feeling of unease in anxiety response, while they block some of the more unpleasant symptoms due to the body's arousal for "fight or flight." They will block, for example, a raised heart rate and raised blood pressure in a stressful situation, as well as tension headache and tremor. As a result they have been popular with sports people who use them to prevent anxiety tremors affecting their billiard game or their golf swing.

The beta-blockers may be useful in the temporary treatment of anxiety symptoms from unavoidable stress because, as we have noted, they do not prevent the warning function of the anxiety response and don't have the same potential for dependence as the sedative drugs. However, they have many unwanted side effects, and should only be prescribed if the anxiety symptoms themselves warrant it. I find propranolol the most useful beta-blocker.

### Treating the symptoms of stage two

The two extra symptoms of stress breakdown caused by fatigue and exhaustion of the body's willpower and inhibitory controls are:

- loss of the capacity for emotional control

- loss of the capacity for self-motivation

59

As these symptoms are due to exhaustion and depletion of the body's resources, the symptoms will abate when the person is rested and the body's reserves are restored. I advise putting overstressed people with exhaustion symptoms into bed and feeding them. They should be encouraged to sleep as long as possible. Food should be high in protein and complex carbohydrates, low in fat. They should be given vitamin supplements, particularly the B group vitamins and extra vitamin C, 500 to 1000 mg per day. I advise extra vitamin C for two reasons: it is an antioxidant, and tends to mop up free radicals, and it plays some part in the body's release of adrenalin and noradrenalin in anxiety. Free radicals are destructive remnants of cell metabolism, like sparks from a furnace. People who have been pushing themselves beyond their limits are likely to generate more free radicals than usual.

## Use of drugs in stage two

The drugs most useful in stage-two stress breakdown are the antidepressant drugs, which are usually prescribed for endogenous depression. These drugs inhibit the enzymes breaking down neurotransmitter substances, and the effect of these drugs is therefore to restore the body's neurotransmitter levels to normal. However, there is no need for antidepressant drugs if an overstressed person's sleep pattern is normal.

Where there is a sleep disturbance—in particular, difficulty staying asleep—the antidepressants should be prescribed in doses similar to those used in endogenous depression. Sedative drugs and ordinary sleeping tablets should not be used, because of the possibility of "out of control" behavior and drug dependence. I prescribe the tricyclic antidepressants doxepin and dothiepen if my patient is having difficulty staying asleep. However, these drugs have side effects and some people find the effects unpleasant.

People who have difficulty getting off to sleep but who can sleep a normal length of time once they do fall asleep, don't need full doses of antidepressants. Their problem is usually that their anxiety symptoms interfere with the ability to relax sufficiently to get off to sleep. In these cases, I usually prescribe only a small dose of doxepin, 10 mg regularly at the same time each night. My aim here is to help my patient get back into normal sleep habits. I have not encountered any significant dependency problem with this drug.

**The newer antidepressants**

Recently, a new family of antidepressant drugs, which increase the levels of the neurotransmitter *serotonin,* have become available. These drugs include fluoxetine (Prozac), paroxetine (Aropax) and sertraline (Zoloft). They have a number of advantages, including safety and an extended range of activity. For example, they seem useful in treating people with obsessive and compulsive symptoms, as well as depression. I have found also that patients with a history of outbursts of rage when they are stressed and overtired, and who have a sleep problem, seem to do well taking fluoxetine.

**Treating the symptoms of stage three**

There are three major symptoms of stage-three stress breakdown:

- intolerance of sensory stimulation
- inability to tolerate things previously tolerated
- apparent change in priorities and attitudes

The symptoms of stage three are caused by the operation of the brain's circuit breakers. These symptoms will disappear when the excessive load on the brain is reduced. However, people experiencing third-stage stress breakdown usually cannot help themselves because the symptoms themselves interfere with the capacity for insight and self-organization. It is useless just giving advice. A rescuer is required.

Almost invariably, people with third-stage stress breakdown symptoms have broken down under a combined load of external and internal stresses. The internal stresses are often a murky web of complex self-contradictory and convoluted demands on the self to look good, not appear vulnerable, and guarantee success. The rescuer will be most helpful when the approach taken is one which bypasses the internal stresses and simplifies and clarifies the task to be dealt with. Something like: "I know how important it has been for you to make sure everything went well. You've worn yourself out doing this, and we are grateful for the contribution and sacrifices you have made. However, if we are to get this project finished we need to focus on those aspects that you personally are responsible for. We won't worry about those things you cannot do anything about."

**Allow the overstressed patient to withdraw**

It is essential for the person with stage-three stress breakdown symptoms to be protected from the added stress of having to explain his unusual behavior. Quiet places providing minimal stimulation are helpful, the best being a quiet bedroom in one's own home, with no telephone. Only consider holiday places if they are quiet and require no great effort on the overstressed person's part. If an overstressed person is to be sent on a holiday, someone else will have to do the bookings and make the travel arrangements.

If the person is admitted to a hospital, there should be no visitors except close family, and these only for short visits.

## Keep explanations simple, avoid misinterpretations

In third-stage stress breakdown, changes in behavior are almost inevitably going to be misinterpreted. The commonest misinterpretation of the symptoms is that of marriage breakdown, as explained in the next chapter. It is essential to explain clearly and simply how the unusual behavior of the overstressed person is caused by stress breakdown. If people close to the overstressed person refuse to accept this explanation, they should be kept away until the situation returns to normal.

## Deep psychotherapy is contraindicated

Psychotherapy or counseling are too stressful for people with stress breakdown symptoms. They cannot process the experience and they will react oddly to the discussion of major problems. I would suggest the following golden rule for counseling: if a person's unusual or abnormal behavior has occurred in a time of high levels of stress or responsibility, that person should not undergo psychotherapy, counseling or joint discussions until properly rested, and relieved of stress.

All methods of psychotherapy impose more stress on the patient, even if it is just the requirement to be somewhere on time for an appointment. Just having to get there and find a parking place might be enough to further disable an overstressed person. As well, most exploratory interviews, no matter how gentle, always include some personal stress.

## Rest, relief of stress, and a lot more sleep

The treatment of a person with stage-three symptoms should include everything already said about the treatment of stages one and two. Rest and relief of stress are the most important things to insist on. We know the healing has started when the overstressed person is overcome by the need to sleep. When someone who has demonstrated unusual behavior in a time of high stress sleeps the whole weekend (without the aid of drugs), this is a very good sign.

## Drugs in third-stage stress breakdown

In general, drugs should be avoided. However, if drugs are used in third-stage stress breakdown, theoretically the best drugs to use would be the antipsychotic drugs used to treat schizophrenic patients, but in small doses, and given only for a short period of time. The drugs which might be useful, would be small doses of chlorpromazine (Largactil), thioridazine (Melleril), trifluoperazine

(Stelazine), or haloperidol (Serenace). ⁷
have troublesome side effects and, w
non-psychotic disorders such as stress ᴅ.
should be used sparingly and for a strictly lim..
time.

We have been looking at the treatment of the
symptoms of stress breakdown. Let us examine now
the treatment of some of the causes of stress breakdown.

## Treating one cause of stress breakdown—coping

We know that stress breakdown occurs because of
one of two basic reasons:

The person has chosen to ignore the warnings of
overload, *or*
The person has been unable to escape from the
stress.

The people who choose to ignore the warning
signals are often people who put a lot of importance
on coping. These people:

- often have high standards which they expect from
  themselves and others

- tend to have low self-esteem and often feel they
  need to earn the approval of others

- tend to use a method of relating to other people
  where they put the needs of other people ahead
  of their own needs

- while they put other people's needs ahead of their

own, may resent having to do this but tend to feel guilty about the resentment they feel

Many factors contribute to these personality traits. From infancy our society is forcing us into competition with others and setting us up for fear of failure. If in addition our parents give us the impression we are loved only if we are successful, we can develop a strong need to guarantee success or else we will not even attempt a task. People who grow up with conditional acceptance in childhood tend to feel bad when things don't turn out as expected, even if what went wrong was something they could do nothing about.

What if you have been a coper for years, and everyone else lets you handle all the problems? You would dearly love to give up your coping addiction but you are fairly certain the rest of the family or the office staff will not let you. Some suggestions:

- Don't stay indispensable for any longer than is absolutely necessary. Insist on someone else being trained to do the work as well.

- Try being unreliable at times when you know it is safe to do so, while they don't. You don't have to let them know this is deliberate. It will do them good to realize they have the capacity to function without you.

- Don't continue with systems that only you can operate.

## Stress we cannot avoid

Many people are in situations where stress is

unavoidable. The mothers of newborn babies cannot hand over sick children readily to someone else. The same often applies to families with severely handicapped members. Police, teachers and ambulance officers find that stress goes with the job. My advice to people in whom stress breakdown seems inevitable:

- If you cannot avoid stress symptoms, understand what they are and don't mistake them for symptoms of illness.

- If you cannot avoid the big problems, let as many non-essentials go as you can.

- Get as much sleep as possible, even if it is just "forty winks" now and then during the day.

- Look after your nutrition. Don't skip meals, or start crash diets.

- Decide to take a holiday when the stress is over, and do it. The holiday might be going to bed for a few days, or going away to recuperate and be pampered.

## New mothers and stress breakdown

Of the many different high stress occupations and situations, I would like to make special mention of the mothers of newborn babies. They often have to cope with stress they cannot avoid, while missing out on sleep. And they have been weakened nutritionally by the metabolic demands of the unborn baby, the effects of the hormones of pregnancy, and sometimes an exhausting labor.

67

The mothers of newborn babies can suddenly develop stress breakdown symptoms, quite often experiencing the three stages at once. This is because their state of health is quite precarious in this postnatal period. Soon after the nervous system begins to warn against overload, with a signal of acute anxiety, these women may break down emotionally because their energy reserves have been seriously depleted. And because of nutritional demands and the fact that the stress on the mother of a newborn baby is often unrelenting, the third-stage switch-off symptoms may follow soon after. Thus the mother can suddenly deteriorate from seeming perfectly normal to appearing very emotionally and mentally disturbed, unable to respond to the baby's needs, simply as the result of stress. Many cases thought to be postnatal depression are in fact cases of serious stress breakdown.

It is usually not difficult to differentiate the postnatal stress breakdown cases from real postnatal depression. Stress symptoms disappear with 48 hours rest, while the symptoms of true postnatal depression persist in spite of rest. The treatment of true postnatal depression is the same as the treatment of endogenous depression occurring at any other time.

I do not agree with the current practice in some obstetric hospitals of sending women home from hospital four days or so after the baby is born. It is sending wrong signals to our society. Hospitals are expensive, noisy and inconsiderate places, and we cannot blame women for wanting to get home to their families as soon as possible. But some women seem to think because they are allowed home they are capable of a normal workload.

Chinese women have the right idea. They have a tradition called "sitting the month": the mother of a newborn baby does nothing other than breastfeed her baby and attend to her own hygiene for one month after the baby is born. While she is being looked after by her husband and others in the family she is recuperating her strength. Traditional Chinese belief is that in this postnatal period, women are vulnerable to all sorts of illnesses because of their weakened condition.

Here is an example of a case of simple stress breakdown in the mother of a newborn baby. Alice and Henry have just moved interstate. They had two children and Alice became pregnant again while they were in a rented house, looking for a house to buy. Their previous house had proved unsuitable when the traffic suddenly became very heavy following a permanent traffic diversion a few blocks away—something they had not foreseen. They had therefore decided to take their time to be sure they made the right choice with their next home. They had their hearts set on a home built of hardwood, set on high stumps, with wide shady verandahs. They did not realize, however, how much work and expense is needed to maintain these homes in good condition.

Just before their baby was born, Alice and Henry found the exact house they were looking for in a leafy quiet street in their preferred suburb. It had a downstairs flat which they moved into as soon as Alice had the baby, while Henry was doing renovations upstairs every night after work. When she could, Alice helped with the painting. The renovations were more expensive and took longer than expected after termites were found in the dining room floor, which had to be replaced. After four months in the flat, Henry and Alice and their three children moved upstairs.

While the family had been crowded into the flat, all of them living in one big bedroom, Alice had felt cramped for room, but it had been cozy with everyone all together. Seeing that it was impossible to keep the flat tidy, she hadn't worried too much about it. The day they moved upstairs, and she saw how much there was to do, Alice suddenly became tense and nervy. She didn't sleep much that night, woke frequently, and next day she found she couldn't face unpacking boxes. She started to lose her temper easily, and would weep at the slightest frustration.

Alice then began criticizing the house, seeing the work still to be done, regretting bitterly they had bought a house that required so much work. She began to experience periods of panic when she realized she was having a nervous breakdown. She asked Henry to stay home from work because she was frightened she couldn't be trusted with the children. Henry rang the doctor.

Important factors in Alice's stress breakdown were:

1. By working at night on the renovations, she had not given herself time to recuperate following the birth of the baby. Her nervous system's processing capacity was impaired by fatigue, and also by depletion because she was breastfeeding.

2. Alice is by nature a perfectionist who fears being unable to cope. In the downstairs flat she had to accept the chaos because there was little she could do about it. Her tasks were finite jobs which she tackled one by one: preparing meals, washing and caring for her children. Upstairs she was suddenly faced with seemingly unlimited tasks which she tended to view as insurmountable. She experienced free-floating anxiety as her nervous system warned her she was incapable of doing all these jobs at once.

3. Alice then became fearful of her own anxiety, immediately recalling her feelings of powerlessness in their previous home, and projected these feelings onto her current situation. She therefore became anxious about being anxious, the basis of panic symptoms.

## Stoicism versus Christianity in vulnerability to overload

The philosophy which demands that we be prepared for all eventualities well in advance so we can bear them with dignity and restraint is that of the Stoic philosophers of the Roman Empire. This Stoic philosophy, far from dying out with the ancient Romans, seems to be alive and well and flourishing as an integral part of modern Western culture.

The best known spokesman for Stoic philosophy was Seneca, one-time tutor to the young Emperor Nero. Nero later forced Seneca to suicide. In his "Letters from a Stoic," Seneca advises his friend:

"Let the personality be made ready to face everything; let it be made to realize that it has come to

71

terrain on which thunder and lightning play, terrain on which

*Grief and vengeful Care have set their couch,*
*And pallid Sickness dwells, and drear Old Age.*

This is the company in which you must live out your days. Escape them you cannot, scorn them you can. And scorn them you will, if by constant reflection you have anticipated future happenings.....We must see to it that nothing takes us by surprise....this habit of continual reflection will ensure that no form of adversity finds you a complete beginner."

The New Testament offers quite different advice:

"This is why I tell you: do not be worried about the food and drink you need to stay alive, or about clothes for your body. After all, isn't life worth more than food? And isn't the body worth more than clothes? Look at the birds flying around: they don't plant seeds, gather a harvest, and put it in barns: your Father in heaven takes care of them! Aren't you worth much more than birds? Which one of you can live a few more years by worrying about it?.....Your Father in heaven knows that you need all these things. Instead, be concerned above everything else with his Kingdom and with what he requires, and he will provide you with all these other things. So don't worry about tomorrow it will have enough worries of its own. There is no need to add to the troubles each day brings." *(Matthew: Chapter 6)*

There are no prizes for guessing which of the two approaches would be better for preventing overload leading to stress breakdown. The problem, however, is the person caught in the middle, who perhaps is afraid to trust God enough to stop worrying about the future, but who believes enough in Christianity to be saddled with a list of do's and don'ts which merely further overload the nervous system.

## Prevention and "the little spacecraft that could"

I am writing this edition of the book on a computer with a memory of 8 megabytes, or 8000K in computer language. I can access any part of the book in moments. The computer I used on the first edition had a memory of 120K, and I could work on only one small chapter at a time. So when I recall that the two Voyager spacecraft which sent back those marvellous pictures of the planets, only have a tiny 16K computer, I feel greatly inspired. Someone dubbed these spacecraft "the little spacecraft that could" after the story of the little train engine that puffed his way up the hill against all odds, one puff at a time: "I think I can, I think I can ...."

So how did the little spacecraft take all the beautiful pictures we see in the National Geographic Magazine? One tiny postage-stamp size at a time. And when that bit is sent back to earth, it is forgotten and the next bit started. Back on earth, a support group of people take the tiny fragments of digitalized messages and put them together into a mosaic. Eventually, a whole picture emerges as the pieces are fitted together.

Busy but effective people function in much the same way, focusing their total attention on what they are doing at the time. They have future goals, but future tasks are for a future time, and forward planning is divided into separate tasks and fitted in a bit at a time.

I think people who cannot believe God exists would have difficulty with this way of working. If the little spacecraft beamed back its tiny pictures to nobody, it would all be in vain. I believe somewhere in the cosmos, the tiny elements of my day are being fitted together into a coherent pattern that makes sense. Sometimes, like looking out of the window of a fast-moving train, the pattern of our lives takes shape only in retrospect, in seeing where we have come.

## A breakdown-proof lifestyle

The basic elements of taking one day at a time, and allowing something greater than the self to integrate our life experiences, are part of the Twelve Steps program of Alcoholics Anonymous, a lifestyle relatively resistant to stress breakdown. It goes something like this:

- I admit my life is in a mess and that I am personally powerless to fix it up.

- There is a power greater than me, and I have come to believe this power might be able to straighten things out.

- I'm going to make a decision to put myself in the hands of God and ask God to take over running my life. I will cooperate with God but, from now on, God will be running things.

- I will talk things over with someone else, make a list of the mistakes I have made, and try to make amends.

- I will have a good look at my gifts and weaknesses and get to know myself better.

- Every day I will say The Lord's Prayer, and when I say "Give me today my daily bread," I am asking for no more or no less than what I need today, my orders for today, and the strength I need to carry out God's instructions for me. I won't ask for more than that. I don't want more than I need, because I would then have to worry about what to do with the excess. I don't want less than I need. Just the day's rations and marching orders, please Lord.

- From now on, I will pay attention to what I am doing at the time, instead of being preoccupied with guarantees for tomorrow.

- Whenever I'm wrong, I will admit it without a fuss, and apologize.

- If something is going wrong, I will ask myself what my motivation is. Am I trying to do the correct thing to the best of my ability? If so, I just have to accept the things that are happening that I cannot alter. The most I can do is pray that God will make the best use of these changed circumstances.

**Time out**

When we have to deal with unremitting stress and suffer anxiety symptoms as a result, we can prevent further stress breakdown by taking little holidays. I think it is better in the long run for an overworked person with a responsible job to take the occasional day off work when feeling overstressed. Even if at the time the person knows he or she really is not sick enough to warrant a day off, occasional time off may prevent a breakdown which could well result in weeks or months away from work. Sensible people in business know that occasional time off may be necessary to keep an employee working at full capacity, especially in high stress occupations.

The office worker should, if possible, get away from the job during the lunch hour, and do something different. Sometimes that little break can be very helpful. A sleep during the lunch hour is even better, if it is possible.

Whatever one's religious beliefs, at least one day of the week should be a day of total rest. This is essential to good mental health. And it is always a good idea for a person with a demanding job to do something on weekends that does not resemble his or her normal work. The intellectual ought to do something requiring physical exercise; the manual worker should do something intellectually stimulating.

## Exercise and relaxation techniques

Most books on stress management recommend physical exercise programs and relaxation techniques to reduce personal discomfort arising from anxiety. I agree. The increase in personal wellbeing and improvements in cardiovascular performance from regular exercise is certainly worth the effort.

Likewise muscle relaxation techniques help to make overstressed people feel a whole lot better.

However, we must remember that anxiety symptoms function as a warning of nervous system overload. It does not make sense to me to concentrate on reducing the discomfort of muscle tension while ignoring the warning of overload. This is like simply covering over the warning light on your car's instrument panel because the red light is bothering your eyes. I find in practice that exercise programs and relaxation techniques do not prevent overstressed people from developing stage two and three stress breakdown symptoms.

Relaxation techniques can be useful in treating the symptoms of stage-one stress breakdown, but when they are effective it is usually because people under stress are obliged to take "time out," to stop doing what they were doing and concentrate on something totally different. I really think that almost any relaxation technique will work so long as it imposes a forced rest.

Likewise, the lunch-time jogging that takes executives away from the desk or the telephone may be effective because it removes them from the source of their stress, rather than simply because of the exercise.

**Meditation**

Some writers on stress management recommend meditation to people who experience a lot of anxiety symptoms. Usually there are two forms of meditation recommended. The first is an active visualization of a pleasant, relaxing scene. You stop what you are doing, get comfortable, and mentally put yourself into a trance-like state, picturing in your imagination a tranquil scene in which you feel completely relaxed and happy. This is more or less self-hypnosis. The other meditation technique involves freeing the mind of ideas and allowing your thoughts, fears, your aches and pains, to lapse into a form of inner silence. At that moment, you are "being," not "doing." After a period of time, you return to your former consciousness, feeling refreshed.

# CHAPTER SIX
## Bullying and Brainwashing

So far we have looked at stress breakdown occurring in response to the ordinary burdens of life. Let us now consider the situation where people break down through being deliberately put under stress by other people:

To punish them—in prisons

To change their way of thinking—in political and religious indoctrination

To destroy their self-confidence—in the persecution of "whistleblowers"

To make them go away—in job restructuring

To enhance the ego of others—in school bullying and domestic violence

## Bullying

Bullying of the powerless by the strong can be seen at all levels in our society. It is often accepted as an administrative method because it appears effective, but in fact it does not work. Organizations who bully their employees are not fully productive. Schools where bullying is rife are inefficient in educating children. And the total cost of domestic violence to our society is enormous.

You will recall that in treating second and third-stage stress breakdown, a rescuer is essential. But where people break down under active harassment, the normal mechanisms that might rescue them cannot operate. For example, school bullies try to stop their victims getting help by threatening even worse violence unless the victim keeps the bullying secret. And exactly the same rules apply in other forms of bullying, including domestic violence.

Where the stress is continuous and the victim is powerless, severe breakdown is inevitable. And where the victim is prevented from reporting the abuse, there is often nowhere else to express their rage except against themselves. This is why depression, self-hatred, self-mutilation and suicide are seen so often in victimized people.

**Handbook on dirty tricks?**

Because of my interest in stress breakdown, I tend to see many victims of active harassment. Often this has occurred in the workplace as part of a deliberate campaign to induce the worker to resign. It is more likely to occur where the harassed worker is hard to get rid of, because of the strength of trade unions or because there is some form of guaranteed tenure, as in the case of universities.

I am always impressed that in different workplaces there is such similarity in the methods that bullies use to break down their victims. It is almost as if they have all sent away for the same handbook on dirty tricks. Then I realize of course that most of these industrial bullies learned their skills as school bullies. They perfected techniques like these in the schoolyard:

- Call the worker to your office for an interview about an alleged failing work performance, but make them wait two hours before seeing them without any explanation. The school bully equivalent is: "Wait until we get you this afternoon after school!"

- Arrange a meeting, supposedly so that several people can provide useful hints on how to help the alleged failing worker. The real aim is, however, to outnumber the worker with several people all finding fault. This is just like the bully and the gang confronting the victim and pretending to be pleasant with something like, "We'd like a little word with you."

- Send the worker for psychological testing or psychiatric interview ostensibly to investigate the reason for an alleged drop in performance, so that some negative label might be applied to the worker. This is similar to the school bully searching for something to tease the victim about, like a family nickname.

- Ignore the worker on the job, and neglect to include the worker and spouse in work-based social functions. Or move the worker to an office without a telephone, and with no work to do. These behaviors are similar to exclusion bullying where the school bully makes sure the group excludes the victim from their games.

- Replace job privileges like the exclusive use of a company car, with the need to share the car with another person who will withhold the car at every opportunity. This is just like the bully having one of his gang take the victim's schoolbag.

- Allow a supervisor to make excessively harsh reports about the worker in language which would previously have been regarded as inappropriate. This is like the bully encouraging one of his gang to rough the victim up.

- Deny the worker access to trade union representation. The school bully usually threatens the victim with increased violence should the victimization be reported.

- Give the worker an excessive workload without any assistance, and then criticize the worker with the inevitable failure to meet deadlines. Bullying is always an unequal contest, with the combined strength of the bully and his gang far outweighing the victim's capacity to respond.

These are just a few examples of workplace bullying, showing how the rules are identical with those of school bullying. When we examine the problem of coercion and victimization in our society we are inevitably faced with the problem of deciding which comes first: bullying in school or bullying in the wider society. Do we tolerate our children bullying other children because we are bullies ourselves at work? Or do we accept bullying at work because we tolerated bullying at school?

In either case, if people are to live in a free society, we must insist that all schools operate effective anti-bullying programs. We need to teach our children that the victimization of the weak by the strong cannot be tolerated.

## Long-term damage from school bullying

The damage to children who are regularly victimized at school extends further than a negative self-image and lack of confidence caused by turning burning resentments against the self. An over-stressed nervous system worrying about how to survive the lunch hour or planning a safer route home from school has little capacity for learning in the classroom. Victimized children do not learn much while they're continually being frightened and humiliated. If the children already have some learning disability which has been siezed upon by the bullies as something to tease about, the chances of succeeding in school are very low indeed.

If it were not for schools, there would not be school bullying. Schools are where children of different sizes and stages of development come together, providing opportunities for the nastier side of human beings to be played out. Schools also function as places where children are graded, assessed, put into groups, rewarded and criticized. Differences between children are maximized, the bright and strong are rewarded, the meek and weak are passed over.

It seems to be an unfortunate fact that schools cannot and do not counteract the effects of victimization. Children who are bullied, and who have learning disabilities as well, have a tendency to fall behind in their education. Some victims of repeated bullying refuse to go to school, others leave at the first chance, but all have their education damaged in some way.

## Different strategies are called for

To help a victimized person who is suffering from stress breakdown, everything in the previous chapters applies, but as well, we must do something to stop the bullying.

In any repetitive pattern of human behavior, some sort of system is operating. Chronic bullying is such a system. The victim keeps the victimization secret, out of fear and shame, the bullies pay no penalty for their behavior, and so they will keep on doing it.

Therefore, the first step in getting free of victimization is to interfere with the system that supports it. The victim has to stop playing the bully's game and change the rules. A woman told me she had always made excuses to cover up for her husband's violence, out of shame and also fear of giving him another excuse to bash her. Then one day someone asked her how she got her black eye and she said, "My husband punched me." It took great courage, but that was the turning point. Once she began reporting his abuse, he lost his control over her.

## New Testament advice

The New Testament contains very effective advice on changing our responses to coercion and harassment:

*If anyone slaps you on the right cheek, let him slap your left cheek too. And if someone takes you to court to sue you for your shirt, let him have your coat as well. And if one of the occupation troops forces you to carry his pack one kilometer, carry it two kilometers. (Matthew 5: 38–41.)*

*Love your enemies, do good to those who hate you, bless those who curse you, and pray for those who mistreat you. (Luke 6: 27–28.)*

What might appear at first sight as stupidity or masochism is actually very sophisticated advice aimed at transforming victims. If a soldier forces you to carry his pack for a kilometer, you become a victim. However, if you were to respond, "No problem. I'll carry it two kilometers," you have immediately become a volunteer, a donor, a helper, someone who can have a relationship with the person making the demands.

## The coin-in-the-jar technique

My favorite method of beating small-order bullying was derived from a direct application of these New Testament principles. It is called the coin-in-the-jar technique. It has been successful in stopping:

- a husband's or wife's regular put-downs at home

- nit-picking criticisms from workmates

- bullying behavior by supervisors

This is how you do it: begin with a little speech, something like this, "Henry, you're a marvellous man, and I realize how much I care about you when you say things that make me feel bad. Because I wouldn't feel so hurt if I didn't care about you so much! So I've decided to save up and buy you something nice. I'm going to remind myself to put 20 cents in this jar every time you say something that makes me feel put down. And when the jar is full, I'm going to use the money in it to buy you something special."

You then do exactly what you said. Every time he says something to make you feel put down, humiliated or ignored, put 20 cents in the jar. This gives you something to do and say in response to the usual negative comments, other than burn silently with resentment or explode in rage. You can say, "That was twice as nasty as what you said this morning. I think that one is definitely worth 40 cents. Henry, you'll have that fishing rod in no time at the rate you're going!"

**I love Henry**
**20 cents per**
**put-down**

*The coin in the jar technique has rarely failed when it is used properly.*

The coin-in-the-jar technique is very effective. Many people stop using behavior they have employed for many years, with five or six coins in the jar. Why is it so successful? Perhaps it provides a totally different response, that of a paymaster paying a servant. It is a response that actually reduces the bullies' status, while appearing to reward them.

Another reason for the technique's success is that it makes the bully slightly anxious. What if his friends heard about this? "I hear Henry's getting paid 20 cents every time he says something nasty to his wife!" This is newsworthy stuff down at the local bar.

One little hint. Henry may try to assert that his statements are not put-downs, they are just true statements. You just say sweetly, "Henry, if I feel bad, they're put-downs to me. And anyway, Henry, you're worth the money!"

When you are using the jar to stop bullying by a supervisor, you might label the jar GOOD ADVICE and alter the speech accordingly. Something like: "I always believe in paying money for good advice, and I'm going to put 20 cents in the jar for every piece of good advice I get. And when the jar is full, the person who has given me the most good advice will get the present."

**The crucifixion experience**

Another concept from the New Testament that is very useful in beating major bullying is that of the crucifixion. The crucifixion of an innocent person is often the means whereby a group of people discover evidence of their own shortcomings. We are beginning to see, through reports from whistle-blowers' action groups, just how corrupt and coercive is the society we live in. We would never have been aware of this if unscrupulous people had not crucified innocent and conscientious workers.

The pattern usually goes like this. A conscientious person refuses to be corrupted by the wrong practices of people around him or her, and refuses to be silent. They are then persecuted by the people doing the wrong thing, metaphorically nailed up and publicly humiliated. However, instead of disappearing, the crucified person survives. At this point, the group tends to split in half. One half questions why this crucifixion is happening: "Why are we persecuting this person? After all, we're the people who have been doing the wrong thing, not him (or her)." The other half maintains their stance of persecuting the innocent person to hide their own corruption, but find they have dwindling support. Conflict between the two groups eventually uncovers the corruption and reform becomes possible. However, for the crucifixion experience to work, it must be public. Mahatma Gandhi understood very well the power of public martyrdom, and used it to initiate reform in both South Africa and India.

I have seen many persecuted but innocent people in my practice, where I have used the crucifixion model to explain what has been happening to them. There is often the potential for a great deal of good to come out of their experiences if they are prepared to allow their persecution to become public knowledge. Although I have to admit this in itself is cold comfort and not much help in stopping the bullying in the short term, it does provide victims with a healthier perspective in which they can stop blaming themselves for their own victimization.

**Winners are grinners?**

Jesus said (Mark 8:35–6) "For whoever wants to save his own life will lose it but whoever loses his life for me and for the gospel will save it." Some people always have to win, and always have to be seen to win. We may be impressed with them for a little while, but as soon as it becomes obvious that their first priority is their own aggrandisement, we lose interest. On the other hand, we admire people who put their own needs last in order to get some project done. And because they will not sing their own praises, we do it for them.

Bullies may generate short-term admiration for their strength, but this popularity will not last long. People who demonstrate integrity and honesty in the face of persecution may be sneered at by a few people to begin with, but in the long term, they will win the approval of many. Victims of political and business bullies need to remember this.

## Brainwashing

The aim of political or religious brainwashing is to force a person to abandon his or her own beliefs and accept uncritically the views of people who have power over them. Most brainwashing techniques induce stress breakdown as rapidly as possible, aiming at producing symptoms of third-stage breakdown. In this state of malfunctioning, the victim finds it difficult to resist indoctrination.

Let us recall two of the symptoms of the third stage, caused by the operation of the circuit breaker mechanisms in relation to overloaded circuits in the nervous system.

**An ability to *not react* to things you have previously tolerated for years. You may become suddenly intolerant of faults and failings in others and in yourself.**

**An apparent personality change. Things you previously regarded as very important in your life now seem to be valued less, while you continue to react normally to trivial matters.**

Patterns of political and religious belief are usually quite complex, made up of things we believe that others do not, and things we do not believe that others do. We usually hold onto these beliefs by psychological processes which include negating other peoples' thinking and overvaluing our own. In third-stage stress breakdown, the ability to use these psychological processes is lost. So under duress we may suddenly change our ideas.

Sometimes this change in ideas brought about by stress can be mistaken for a true religious conversion experience. William Sargant's book *Battle for the Mind* describes many examples. Sometimes we regard the outcome of a successful stress-induced attitude change as acceptable. No doubt the audience in Shakespeare's day approved of the changed Kate in *The Taming of the Shrew*. A late-twentieth-century feminist audience may not be so approving.

The different elements employed to enforce Kate's "taming" or attitude change can be readily identified in many cases of religious "conversions." I personally believe true religious conversions take place all the time. They come about quietly through a deep inner change, and external circumstances have little other than a triggering effect. On the other hand, many cases of so-called conversions which occur under conditions of stress are really examples of religious brainwashing.

Let us examine some common elements in enforced attitude change:

1. The subject or victim is removed from his own familiar surroundings to an unfamiliar place. This

immediately increases the load on the brain's processing capacity through having to adapt to changed circumstances for every activity normally done automatically at home like showering and eating. Many so-called conversions that later wear off occur on church camps. Kate's conversion occurred after she was taken to Petrucchio's house.

2. Through some form of strenuous activity a state of fatigue is induced. In Kate's case this was an exhausting journey, in others it may be hours of singing, dancing or exercise.

3. Stress breakdown is induced through enforced waiting, fear, being denied food, sleep deprivation, deliberately confusing the subject, and forcing decisions to be made on conflicting data and then instantly reversed. Remember how Kate was forced into making conflicting statements about the moon versus the sun, under threat of Petrucchio's violence.

4. The changed attitudes or beliefs are then rewarded, in Kate's case with high praise as she publicly demonstrated her new-found obedience towards her husband.

These elements are also present in many well-known political interrogation techniques. They are all conditions which impose a processing strain on the human nervous system, as set out in the earlier chapters. Things Kate did not have to endure might include threats, torture, and the use of drugs and electroshock.

Exhaustion is hastened by encouraging the victim to use his willpower to resist the will of the interrogator. A clever interrogator will appear impressed by his victim's ability to tolerate pain, and will pretend to be losing heart, to encourage the victim to commit more and more inner resources in a game of fruitless resistance. The aim of this is to cause second-stage breakdown as soon as possible, so as to move on quickly to third-stage symptoms.

It is important, then, to understand the relationship of stress breakdown and enforced attitude change.

In conclusion, it must be emphasized that a free society should have no place for situations where innocent people break down because they are deliberately put under stress. Coercion and victimization are serious problems that must be addressed.

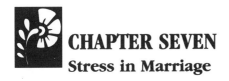

# CHAPTER SEVEN
## Stress in Marriage

Two noticeable features of our society in recent years are the high divorce rate and the increasing number of one-parent families. I believe that stress breakdown is responsible for the failure of many marriages. In many cases, seemingly rock-solid marriages fail to withstand the effects of excessive stress, even where the stress was external to the relationship. Let us see why.

Three main characteristics of a good marriage are:

1. A good sexual relationship
2. Personality differences. We marry people who have qualities we lack
3. Things in common, like sense of humor and political views

As described in Chapter four, the three symptoms of third-stage stress breakdown, caused by the operation of the brain's circuit breakers, are:

1. Avoidance of sensory stimulation
2. Intolerance of differences which are normally accommodated
3. Apparent change in personality and priorities

It is thus easy to see why so many couples experiencing the symptoms of stress breakdown can suddenly think that their love relationship is at an end. A good sexual relationship is difficult when you are avoiding sensory stimulation! And suddenly the endearing personality differences that once fascinated and intrigued you have become utterly irritating and intolerable. On the other hand, for the partner, communication is difficult because the stressed person no longer seems to feel as strongly about the big questions as before. This overstressed person is a stranger to you now. You used to know exactly how he or she would react to a joke or a planned outing. Not any more.

A strong lasting marriage requires a great deal of tolerance on both sides. Even the strongest marriages, where partners do not have unreal expectations of each other or unresolved problems associated with their parents, are really put to the test by stress breakdown. Marriages already vulnerable don't stand much chance at all.

## Two main models for marriage

There seem to be two major models for marriage in our society. There is the traditional marriage based on Christian concepts, now being strongly challenged by the modern de facto marriage based on a concept of democratic sharing.

The de facto marriage begins when a young man and a young woman live together in an intimate relationship, with the intention of sharing everything, including parental responsibilities, on the basis of an equal 50/50 split.

Unfortunately, surveys show that this hoped-for 50/50 sharing does not happen. It has been found, for example, that women do more housework and take more responsibility for children than men, even when both are employed full time in similar jobs. This applies even when the males believe they are sharing the responsibilities equally.

The traditional Christian marriage is based on an ideal of romantic love and complementary role differences, with the marital union blessed by God. A central concept is that the relationship between husband and wife is the same as that between Jesus Christ and His Church. This is prefigured in the Jewish notion that God is to Israel as bridegroom is to bride. What this actually means in day-to-day living can be deduced from examining how Christians in general relate to Jesus Christ in the spiritual life of the Church.

Here is how this traditional ideal marriage was often translated into marital roles:

**HE** loved his wife unconditionally, to the extent of being willing to sacrifice his life for her if necessary. He provided, sustained and protected. In his own mind, and in his influence on the children, he elevated his wife to a level of goodness and purity that she would be unable to sustain without his help and protection. He always forgave, and he never demanded anything from his wife that she would not willingly give of her own accord.

**SHE** was loyal to her husband at all times. Even though her affections might vary, she respected him, and his profession and station in life. She allowed her husband to protect her and the children. She never put the family in danger by moving away from that protection. She loved freely and openly. She was a source of cheer and comfort to all the people she knew. In response to her husband's love, she too loved unconditionally, holding nothing back in her love relationship with her husband. She never left her husband out of any major decisions she made.

**THEIR** sexual relationship brought a union in spirit between the two, affirming the love between them, with the possibility of creating new life.

**THEY,** both husband and wife, submitted to the possibility that their love might lead them to responsibilities, attachment, loss, joy and sorrow, over which, individually, they might have little control.

It is obvious that the husband and father's role in the traditional Christian concept of marriage is very different from the modern de facto marriage based on equality. If the husband is to be like Christ, and the wife like the Church, the support is always going to be one way: always from him to her. As a Christian I feel loved by God; and empowered by this never-failing support, I can respond by loving others. In the same way, the wife in the traditional concept will always be able to rely on her husband's constant support, and this guarantee of support will give her the self-assurance to be a support for her children and others.

But can the situation be reversed? Can the husband always rely on his wife's never-failing support when he is feeling sorry for himself? In reality, not for long. A woman seems to have difficulty knowing what to say to her husband when he has lost his self-confidence. This is in contrast to her capacity to stand by a man who has been physically afflicted with some severe disability, providing of course that he himself doesn't lose hope and demonstrates a minimum of personal courage.

In my experience, a wife's emotional support for a husband who has lost his self-confidence is usually provided through enrolling him temporarily as an honorary child. She then mothers him for as long as it takes. And while the wife is mothering the husband the sexual relationship is likely to be seriously affected.

Usually, the wife soon becomes intolerant of her husband's lack of self-confidence, and may resort to taunting him with exhortations like "Why can't you be a man?" Modern husbands who believe in marriage as equal sharing and mutual support feel shocked and betrayed when their wives respond to their emotional despondency not with sympathetic encouragement, but with stinging insults. What is worse, these modern husbands can see for themselves that their wives would never say such nasty things to their children or their own relatives. Their previous faith in women is shattered. In my experience, when these men seek professional help, they often reveal that they have lost respect for their wives.

### When he is down, she attacks him? Why?

It is a common observation that when a man loses his self-confidence his wife will attack him, sooner or later. It is one characteristic of female behavior that women themselves despise. Women have been talking to me about this for years, saying things like, "I know he can't help losing his business with the recession and all, but I can't seem to be able to stop picking on him. I think I must be a bad-tempered bitch with an attitude problem!"

No doubt some people will argue with me on this point. Some claim this does not happen, and they can give me examples of women who have tirelessly supported a relatively useless husband for years. However I usually find that these cases quoted to me in rebuttal are classic examples of dysfunctional families where a codependent woman has continually mothered an addicted man, to the ultimate detriment of both of them.

Those who believe in the traditional Christian model of marriage can see why a woman with children will not know how to support her husband emotionally when he falls in a heap. After all, according to the Christ/husband—Church/wife analogy, he is supposed to take care of her. Imagine that all the Christians all over the world simultaneously received the same message in prayer: that Christ had lost his nerve, developed low self-esteem, and now did not feel confident about the future? How would Christians approach the problem of trying to restore the Lord's self-confidence? We would be lost and frightened indeed.

In fact, a mother *does* feel lost, frightened, and unsure what to do when her husband cannot help himself. It was always so, back at the beginning of human existence.

## The way we were

Look at human beings now, and try to visualize how it was before the Stone Age in Africa, where we presumably originated. We are ground-dwelling creatures without claws, fangs or camouflage. We are not fast runners, climbers, diggers or swimmers. Children up to the age of 12 years are like meals for the taking by predators like leopards or lions or hyenas. And yet we survived, and totally overran the planet.

One of the main factors in our survival has been the single-minded commitment of mothers to the safety of their children. A woman with children puts the children's survival first. Her own survival is next, because she knows that nobody else will look after her children as well as she does, and they may not survive without her.

On countless occasions the survival of families has depended upon a woman's willingness to walk away from a broken man, to take herself and her children to a safe place where their needs can be met. This is still the case; modern women still become fearful when their husbands cannot help themselves or will not commit themselves to the family's support. These mothers take the children and go.

In stone-age cultures, life could take a sudden dangerous turn if the father, hunter and protector were suddenly unable to stand or walk. Firstly, he would not be able to hunt and they might starve in the winter. Secondly, he would not be able to protect himself or them from predators. As soon as she suspected he could not help himself, she tested him out. If she proved he was out of action by his inability to stand up to her taunts and accusations, she would leave him as soon as possible and hurry for shelter elsewhere.

## Self-sacrifice in men

The instinctive behavior of a woman taking her children and walking away from her broken man has a counterpart in male instinctive behavior. Men have a tendency to react to their own failures by sending their wives and children away to a place of safety. This capacity for self-sacrifice in men is quite real, and they are usually sincere when they perceive themselves to be no longer useful and say something like "I've had it, I'm no good to you any more. I think you should take the kids and go to your mother's."

This capacity for self-sacrifice is evident in the way men are consistently overgenerous in the early months of separation leading up to property settlement in divorce cases. Lawyers often warn their male clients about this, and I, too, have had to do so many times over the years. After a few months, the man may come to regret his early self-sacrificing generosity.

## Some advice for "hen-pecked" men

This advice is for hen-pecked husbands only: When your wife is continually criticizing you and pointing out your faults, remember she is a woman, and women do not usually enjoy putting people down as much as men do. The reason she is doing this is that she is frightened she may be tied to a loser and that the whole family is in danger of being plunged into poverty. She is scared, and so she attacks, but her bark is worse than her bite. Although she may deny it, what she wants is for you to brighten up and exercise some authority in your family.

To prove this, all you have to do is change your response, mentioning success. For example: "Alice, don't speak to me like that! When we are successful, rich and famous, I won't be able to take you along to important social functions if you are going to speak like that."

I believe nagging women are looking to their husbands to provide hope. You do not have to be an overnight success to have your wife call off her attacks. You just need to be able to give her some reason to believe in you, and to give her a little bit of praise.

**Equality in marriage has not happened**

In my experience in clinical psychiatry, it seems that the modern ideal of 50/50 sharing just does not happen. I often have to counsel men disillusioned by the disloyalty of their wives towards them. They say they are always making sacrifices for their family, and they are expected to be supportive whenever anyone is ill or frightened. Yet when they are feeling down, they might get some encouragement from their wives for a day or so, but then they are likely to receive a stern dressing-down for being "whining wimps."

I have found these modern fathers are relieved to learn they are not unique. They feel much better about the inequalities in their marital relationship when their situation is examined in the context of the traditional Christian marriage with differentiated roles. Does it not feel right for your wife to put the safety of the children first? When she is scared because you have lost your nerve, doesn't this reaffirm how important you are in supporting and protecting her? Would you really like to be married to a woman whose standards are so low she will accept a no-hoper as the father of her children?

## Sharing at a deep level with your spouse?

I think one of the most misunderstood aspects of married life is the difficulty husbands and wives have in sharing deep feelings. Many married people seek advice because they have found it easier to discuss deep and meaningful topics with others than with their spouse. Convinced there must be something wrong, they may enrol in weekend marriage enrichment workshops and seminars. The central idea of many of these seminars is a modern myth that we have lost the art of communicating at a deep level—as though we have forgotten to let our spouses in on our deep feelings, while we are perfectly capable of sharing these with friends or even total strangers.

Over the years I have seen many people return from these seminars full of the marvelous things they have learned about each other, only to lapse in the following months back into their former husband and wife truce. It is very much like the dieter, suddenly slender with a conversion to sensible eating and power walking, who steadily fills out as the memory of the last crash diet fades.

One reason why these marriage enrichment seminars wear off is that in most cases there never was a communication deficit at all. Husbands and wives who have been best friends for many years often keep their deep thoughts to themselves for good reason. For example, we have just been discussing one of the reasons why husbands learn to keep their fears to themselves. Moreover, sensible people realize that we project too many of our problems from our families of origin onto the persons we love, so it is often best to keep our comparisons to ourselves.

Often the truth is exactly the opposite of the notion that we have lost the art of communication. It is *because* we love each other that we sometimes decide it is safer not to communicate our deeper feelings. In my experience when there is a real difficulty in communication between husband and wife, there is usually some malfunction causing it, such as stress breakdown or mental illness.

## Expectations of marriage partners

It is commonly recognized that husbands and wives take into marriage a lot of false expectations about each other, originating in their families of origin. We all fall in love with our mothers in that bonding period soon after birth. And little girls can fall in love with their fathers as well. When we fall in love as adults, we bring all those childhood feelings and fears associated with our experiences of love, and project them onto the person to whom we have given our heart. We have also grown up in a household where we witnessed adults interacting with each other, and we tend to bring along expectations of how husbands and wives should interact.

People who have had the privilege of communicating on a deep level with human beings get to know something of the way the unconscious mind works. We find that the unconscious mind does not differentiate between images of the father, the husband, and the eldest son. They all seem to be filed away in a big box in the unconscious mind, labelled "significant male." Likewise the husband's unconscious mind lumps together his mother, his wife, and perhaps his eldest daughter, in one box labelled "significant female."

For this reason, many couples find themselves accusing each other of things that each of them in fact, does not do. "You're always complaining!" accuses the husband (whose mother was always complaining). "When have I complained?" responds his wife. "I can't remember just now, but I know you're always doing it!" he answers. In reality, it was his mother who was always complaining, and his unconscious mind has identified his wife with his mother.

Distortions such as these are commonplace, the cause of a great deal of mystifying confusion during discussions between spouses about their problems in relating to each other. Fortunately, some intelligent couples are able to work out for themselves that they have been accusing each other of behavior which is in reality the former behavior of a parent.

Every normal marriage has to withstand a number of these false expectations based on behavior in families of origin. Stress breakdown seriously interferes with the couple's ability to handle these misconceptions and, as well, interferes with the ability to discuss them rationally.

## Stress and sex

We are discussing how stress could impact on normal marriages. Many of the arguments that occur in marriages under stress are about sex. It is my experience that these arguments almost entirely arise from men's ignorance about female sexuality. And most of the problems would disappear if men would only listen to what their wives are trying to tell them.

Women often complain that in relation to sexual behavior men are incredibly stupid. She explained it all in detail to him last time: what turns her off, what she likes and does not like. But he now seems to have forgotten it all.

From his perspective, he often does not understand what she is talking about. Yes, he does remember that she explained it all to him last time they had the same argument, but he forgot what she said. He forgot it because what she said didn't fit in with his view of how a relationship should be. Men often see female sexuality as full of contradictions. For example:

- If he's passionately interested in her, she's interested,
- But if she feels pressured, she is instantly turned off.
- She is impressed if he is self-confident,
- But if he boasts, she is not impressed.
- She likes him to praise her,
- But if she thinks he's insincere, she feels humiliated.

An intelligent husband never mentions sex to his wife when he desires to take her to bed, because if she is not sexually aroused at the time she usually finds the idea repugnant. The only parts of her anatomy he describes as desirable to press against him are her lips. The only part of his anatomy he describes as throbbing with desire is his heart. If he attempts to use tricks, techniques and routines, she will see through him. Genuine respect is the most important factor in a good sex life.

## Can he be trusted?

Impatient men, who would want sex served up on demand like fast food, are not happy that there is always some sort of obstacle course to be negotiated before mating takes place. In the animal world, it's simple: the female indicates interest in mating, the males fight, and the best male wins her.

A woman is more likely to be interested in a man who is self-confident and capable, and willing to commit himself emotionally to her. So he needs to prove to her that he is interested in her personally, not just as a sex object; that he is self-confident and he is sincere.

Sincerity is important because she wants to know he can be trusted. Women who are sexually aroused tend to lose control of their emotions and become totally available. Men, by contrast, do not lose emotional control during orgasm to the extent that women do. Therefore a woman is quite vulnerable to being controlled by a man within their sexual relationship.

## Sex and prayer?

If we accept the traditional Christian concept that Christ is to the Church as husband is to wife, then we can find explanations for a number of problem areas in male/female relationships. For example, intimate lovemaking is equivalent to deep prayer, wherein the soul enters into a deep, intimate relationship with God.

So if you want some really good sex with your spouse, make your preparations as if you were preparing to relate to God on a deep level. Think of things you might do to draw closer to God, and do and say those things to your partner. Jesus told us not to worry too much about what actual words we say in prayer. Just form a loving intention in your heart and God hears the prayer anyway. So do not worry too much about your sexual performance, about pressing button A and then moving on to lever B. Just concentrate on revealing physically how much you love each other. Nature will take care of the details.

This sort of advice is what many women have been unsuccessfully trying to tell their husbands for years. They want to feel special—they don't want to be handled like a machine to be operated in a particular sequence—they want the sexual fulfilment to occur as part of a loving intimate experience.

## Commitment

In discussing aspects of the sexual relationship in traditional marriage, and some concerns of women about their potential for losing control, we can include the area of commitment to family. It seems that women in traditional marriages voluntarily surrender their individual sovereignty for about fifteen years after they marry. Then at about age 37, they may begin to wonder, "Who am I, apart from being someone's wife and someone else's mother? What opinions are mine, coming from me?"

Sometimes these women are frightened by this exploration of self, worrying that this new-found unwillingness to be just "Mum" means their marriage is at an end. Sometimes the husband will start worrying as well, and resist her fledgling attempts to redeem her own individuality. Sadly, misunderstandings on both sides can sometimes lead on to family breakdown, which could have been prevented if the husband had helped and encouraged his wife to explore the individuality she so lovingly surrendered for the sake of the family.

## Male territoriality

I often explain to women that if they could get inside their husbands' heads and look out through their eyes, they would see the world as a very different place: a world marked off in boundaries, with complex hierarchies of dominance and importance; a world with complex rules aimed at avoiding conflict.

For example, a man is walking down a long corridor when he sees a familiar face coming towards him. He is trying to identify this person, and in doing so, he looks at this man's eyes a moment too long, before he realizes that the other person resembles a popular movie star and he does not really know him at all. Because he has now "eyeballed" the stranger, this represents an aggressive challenge, and he is obliged to offer some form of greeting with an explanation for looking too long. If he does not make some appeasement gesture, he will risk having created an enemy.

I have found that women often underestimate how touchy men can be when their authority is challenged or their belongings are used without permission. This is often the cause of unnecessary arguments.

While men and women are equal in intelligence, they look and behave very differently. These differences are to a large extent due to the effects of male and female sex hormones on the brain, and appear to be designed to equip men emotionally for hunting and killing and protecting their families, and women for nourishing, caring for and educating children.

In stone-age communities, men were the hunters and women were the food gatherers. These activities require different skills. Hunters needed to coordinate their activities, going out in groups for mutual protection. They needed to be tough-minded and able to kill. Skilful hunters could anticipate the movements of the animals they were hunting, estimating their approximate whereabouts from observations of the speed and direction the animals were moving. It is said that men are better at reading road maps than women, and that they navigate mainly by a process of dead reckoning, where you work out where you are by how fast you travelled for how long.

Women were the food gatherers. They went out together for protection, but it was not necessary for their activities to be coordinated, as in hunting. Food gathering requires well-developed powers of observation and a memory for where things are. Because fruit does not move, it is not necessary to pick the first lot of fruit encountered. There might be a tree with riper fruit, and the tree with less ripe fruit can do for another day. It was also important for women gathering food to notice other foods that they would remember and come back for at another time. It is said that women are better than men at remembering landmarks. They seem also to be better at remembering where things are at home.

## Shopping: hunting versus food gathering

The difference between male and female approaches to obtaining food can be clearly seen today in our attitudes to shopping. Men go out hunting when they go shopping. Buying a pair of shoes is accomplished in much the same way as going out to spear a wild animal. Go to where the shoes are, get a pair, and take them home.

Women are usually very scathing about such behavior. They insist you should look in all the other shoe shops to make sure you have bought the most suitable shoes available. And they are irritated by the male insistence on returning home immediately with the purchase. For women, shopping is food gathering, and all the ancient rules apply: look around, check out all the bargains, make a mental note of goods that might do for Christmas presents next year.

Men and women out shopping together are a very volatile mix. Arguments often start in shopping centers. Men cannot tolerate the way women, en route to some purchase, will suddenly stop and look at something totally unrelated to what they came for. Some men prefer to trail their wives, keeping a few paces behind, having learned from the experience of suddenly finding their wives are fifty meters behind, and having to turn around and go back for them. However, this situation of having your husband always a few paces back and out of normal conversation range, is intensely irritating to women. I see it as an example of a classic no-win situation.

Women become really annoyed with husbands who buy the first thing that fits their description of what they want, when the shop next door had something much more suitable at a cheaper price. On the other hand, men become highly irritated with the female insistence that you must never buy the first thing you see, on principle. How many men have secretly stifled a delicious "I told you so" after following women around comparing products only to find when they get back to the first store, that the last of the desired items has been sold?

## The Zen Garden

Do you think stress has affected your marriage? Are you thinking you would like to try to sort out some of the misunderstandings? Let me tell you about the Zen Buddhist rock gardens in Japan. On a square of raked gravel there might be eleven large rocks, so placed that from whatever side you look you cannot see them all. People looking from different sides will see a different number of rocks. Only heaven, looking down from above, can see all the rocks at once. The garden's simple message is that no single view of reality is valid.

Men and women are very different in the way they view exactly the same set of circumstances. Husband and wife are going to see different versions of the same truth. And only heaven, looking down from above, will see the whole truth. As in a Zen garden, couples looking from different sides, but accepting each other's statements as valid, and comparing notes in a spirit of cooperation, may be able to work out how many rocks there are.

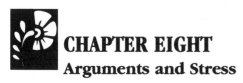 **CHAPTER EIGHT**
## Arguments and Stress

Couples under stress can spend a lot of time arguing. But then again, that is true in general of a lot of men and women who love one another. When couples report they never argue at all, I usually find someone has been giving in all the time for the sake of peace. And a one-sided peace does not last very long.

In my experience, the subject that people most argue about is arguing itself. They argue about why they cannot communicate. In our well-educated equal-opportunity society we would not anticipate major communication difficulties between men and women. Yet many couples find it hard to understand each other and to realize that both men and women have their own, quite different, bargaining and negotiating method.

## Differences in negotiating styles

### Women begin with an up-front overstatement

Women begin with an up-front approximate overstatement

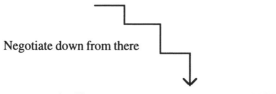

Negotiate down from there

And hope to come to some agreement NOW

I have found that many men are not aware that women tend to put the emphasis at the beginning of a discussion, with an up-front overstatement that is only approximately related to the matter being discussed. There is usually some decision to be made, and women tend to think all they really need to do is spark the discussion and the process of talking about it will produce an agreement *now*.

## Men begin with a vague understatement

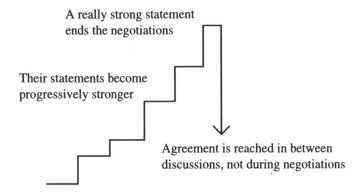

A really strong statement ends the negotiations

Their statements become progressively stronger

Agreement is reached in between discussions, not during negotiations

Men on the other hand, usually begin a discussion with a vague understatement by one of them, gradually escalating the tension and the clarity of his demands, and watching the other man's reaction carefully. He has to decide how far to push his claim. A strong statement will either produce a violent reaction or will end the negotiations. The strong statement "I'm afraid it is 10% or nothing!" is likely to end the discussion. The reply might be: "In that case I'll have to talk to my people and get back to you." If a decision is made, it is made in between discussions. A later phone call: "We had a look at your proposal and we feel we can't possibly go over 9%." This might be acceptable: "I think my people will accept that." Women often become irritated by the long drawn-out process of male negotiating. They are interested in coming to some agreement now, not at some indefinite time in the future.

Why should there be such a marked difference in negotiating styles between men and women? I am sure the answer can be found in role differences. Many behavioral characteristics of women make sense when we see them caring for children. The nutritional and educational needs of children are immediate, and when a problem arises, it needs to be settled now, not later. When rescuing children from danger, a woman does not have to pay attention to the exact words she is saying. The important part is the fact of intervening. It does not really matter how you tell a child the fire will burn him, so long as you say it loud, with feeling. Thus the emotionally charged up-front approximate overstatement which initiates an instant discussion and decision, has evolved in the context of women having primary responsibility for the care and safety of children.

On the other hand, men have always been responsible for the safety of the overall family or community. They need to be on the lookout for predators, to be able to discern the men who can be trusted from those who cannot, and to be able to coordinate their efforts in hunting and farming. It has therefore been important for men not to reveal their feelings or their intentions too early in negotiations, and not to upset their male peers, on whom they rely for help.

These differences have been summed up by a

medical friend of mine as women possessing prox-
imal intuition, and men distal intuition. Women in
general seem more likely to know intuitively what
is needed now, while men generally appear to have
a better intuitive awareness of the medium term
results of actions taken now.

There are now more women in middle management than ever before, many of whom are
unaware they are using a different negotiating
method from the men they are supervising. I have
had to counsel a number of males who were upset
over the up-front overstatements of their female
supervisors. My advice includes an assumption that
verbal criticism from a female supervisor will tend
to be more scathing than will appear in the written
report, whereas with male supervisors the opposite
will be true. Men tend to minimize their criticisms
in initial verbal communication, but the later written report will contain what the male supervisor
really thinks.

This up-front overstatement of women at the
beginning of a discussion is very confusing to men.
Men tend to see strong statements as having been
thoroughly thought out before they are said,
because for men a strong statement comes at the
end of a discussion and is mainly used to define the
differences that remain between the two parties. So
when a woman thinks she is opening up a discussion with a statement like, "I think we're heading for
divorce!", her husband believes she has thought
long and hard about this and is defining her position, and he might answer with, "That'd be right!" As
far as he is concerned, that's the end of the discussion. He expects they'll think about it separately and

open the discussion later with an altered position statement.

## The softly-softly approach

I have had many discussions with women who report their husbands are not interested in discussing their marital differences. Each time she has tried to open a discussion, he says she has obviously made up her mind and there is no sense trying to talk her out of it. She is completely baffled by this response because she hasn't made up her mind at all. When I have been able to convince the woman to tone down her opening statements the husband's response is gratifyingly different. This is particularly true if she can give her husband an idea of what she wants. For example: "Henry, if you've got a minute, I'd like to talk to you about what rules we should insist on for the kids when they go into the city on Friday nights. I'd like you to hear what I'm feeling about it. I don't need you to make up my mind. Then I'd like to hear what your opinion is."

This approach usually works. Much more acceptable than her previous attempt at beginning the conversation: "Why don't you care if our kids get mugged on Friday nights?" I have to say, however, that women usually find it hard to abandon the short, pungent approximation for the more rambling and wordy male opening statement. They usually claim they don't have the time to waste.

## Keep talking

My advice for the man who cuts short a discussion with his wife because he mistakenly thinks she has made up her mind and is unlikely to change it, usually goes something like this: "Your wife expects you are going to try to talk her out of it." Some men are quite surprised to hear this, and rather relieved at the next piece of advice: that there is a strong likelihood his wife was using an approximate statement to open the conversation, and her opening remarks are negotiable. Many men have been behaving as though they did not have a right to question their wives' opening statements, and have been pleased to find out they are expected to put up some opposition if they do not agree.

## Men and women talk for different reasons

They were driving along in the car. Nothing had been said for a few minutes. Then she said, "If we'd gone the other way we'd be there by now." He asked himself why she'd say such a thing.

Men communicate with each other either to convey information or to score points off one another in competitive wordplay. They pay close attention to the words used and tend to answer questions word for word. So he wondered if she was trying to score points, or was she telling him something he needed to know? But women often communicate just to show solidarity or sympathy, or even to break a silence, and therefore the actual words used may not be as important as the fact of communicating. Was she simply making conversation, or was she telling him something important, so on the next trip they might take the other road? Either way he was irritated, but he knew she wouldn't understand why.

Men react badly to female "postmortem" statements like:

"You should have gone the other way."
"You shouldn't have bought the first TV you saw."
"You shouldn't have taken that parking spot, here's one a lot closer."
"You should have told her we didn't want it if it had a scratch on the door."

To them it seems as though the woman is acting as prosecutor, judge and jury, has reached her verdict and announced her decision. Since she has found the prisoner guilty of taking the wrong road, he expects that nothing he might say in his defense will save him. The verdict has already been reached.

## I just want you to know how I feel

Women have often expressed irritation at not being allowed by their husbands simply to let their emotions out, to say what they feel. A man is often unaware his wife may open a conversation simply to express her feelings, without any thought of asking him to do anything about the problem. More than anything she wants some affirmation that it is understandable to feel that way, that she's not neurotic or selfish or being silly because she feels so upset.

Women should understand that men have difficulty in this area, and if a woman wishes to raise an emotive issue she should state clearly what response she is seeking from her husband.

Many emotive utterances of men evolved as a means of frightening off competitors without having to resort to violence. Therefore men tend to regard ambiguous emotive statements as probably hostile, and react accordingly.

## Men and women use words differently

Men and women may use certain words differently—e.g. *always* and *never*. Women tend to use always to describe a recurring event, as "in the old days Grandad was always fishing," whereas men use always as meaning "every single time without exception." To women, never is the negative of always, whereas to men, never is a very strong word which strictly means "not at any time since the dawn of history."

Furthermore, women tend to use some words very carelessly—words which to men have specific functions—such as *why?* and *how?* To men, why? means "please give me a verbal explanation now." And how? usually means "please outline now the method you are going to use." This difference in word usage is very important, as in the following scenario:

> She: You never wash the dishes!
> He: I hope you remember I washed up last Thursday night.
> She: Exactly! The defense rests!
> (He is speechless, flabbergasted.)
> She: When did you wash up before that?
> (He cannot remember.)
> She: See! You *never* wash up!

## Unanswerable questions

Many men complain their girlfriends seem to expect them to have a working knowledge of advanced motivational theory, when they are required to answer such questions as:

"Why is it you never tell the truth when you say you love me?"
"If you're going to look at other women, why did you ask me out?"
"How come you never listen to a word I say?"
"Why aren't you ever here when you're really needed?"
"Why are you always making excuses?"

The men may attempt to answer these questions, word for word. However, their vague, abstract but quite sincere attempts are usually regarded as unsatisfactory and evasive by their girlfriends who have simply used language carelessly. I have often heard women say, "You know what we mean!" In fact, men have very little idea of what they mean.

## Whoever loses the fight must leave the area

Among higher animals, conflict over authority, over who's the boss, runs according to certain rules. Usually a submission gesture stops the fight, the loser leaves, and the bystanders are required either to recognize the successful challenger, or to reaffirm the status of the previous boss who has successfully fought off the challenge. The same rules apply with human beings, and they can be seen in operation in a political leadership challenge as well as in family arguments.

Knowing these rules, it is easy to see that the person who angrily leaves the house, driving off in the car or going for a walk, has lost an argument over authority. If this happens regularly the indication is that this person feels he or she does not have a place in the family, and I always regard it as an ominous sign of future family breakdown.

## Teenagers are programmed to challenge their parents

I have been surprised to find how many women are unaware that teenagers are programmed to challenge the authority of their parents. In males it is associated with the hormone testosterone. The teenage boy becomes uncooperative and surly, and begins to mutter criticisms of his father. Surprisingly, the mother is often not aware that this challenge is normal for a teenage boy.

Many men feel their authority is under threat from feminism, and have been overreacting to challenges to their authority in recent years. When the father overreacts to the challenge of his teenage son, the mother does not support him. She says something like, "I cannot support a man who's so nasty to his own children!"

The father, wrongly thinking his wife knows full well that the son is merely mounting a routine teenage authority challenge, feels she has actively joined the son's rebellion. He wonders why, and concludes she herself is using this as an opportunity to challenge his authority. In this frame of mind, he overreacts all the more to the son's surliness, and the mother becomes increasingly critical of her husband's behavior. The situation worsens and, if the father believes he is outnumbered, he will consider leaving home.

I have advised many a woman over the years to

leave Dad and the kids to sort out their differences without her interference. This is, of course, assuming that Dad is a normal father, and that the relationship problems are not due to some pathological process like alcoholism or mental illness.

## Stress symptoms or adolescent behavior?

This might be an appropriate place to discuss the contribution of stress symptoms to behavior that we often assume is just a part of adolescence. A lot of disturbed behavior in teenagers is in fact caused by stress breakdown, but too often we don't recognize it. Examples of such behavior are explosive displays of emotion, ignoring big problems while being preoccupied with trivia, and wanting to be left alone. If we fail to recognize these behaviors as symptoms of stress breakdown, we may unknowingly put even more stress on our teenagers by reacting inappropriately.

Teenagers are vulnerable to stress breakdown because of the nature of the problems they have to deal with. They have to resolve many big questions by crisis, by a "leap in faith" mechanism, throwing all their energy into something without knowing for sure what the outcome might be.

For example, some teenagers may have to make a commitment to study or a training program for perhaps six years. They don't know enough about themselves or the chosen career at that time to be certain they will enjoy the work when they eventually finish their training. Their choice of life partner, and perhaps of political ideology, are made in the same way. It is all nerve-racking stuff. At the same time they are at the mercy of hormone changes affecting their emotions, and are trying to cope with unavoidable personal and sexual problems.

## Why people with stress breakdown symptoms are likely to become involved in arguments

People who have learned to recognize stress breakdown symptoms can usually tell when arguments in the family are stress-related. In the first stage, when overstressed people are suffering from the symptoms of anxiety, disputes may arise because they are preoccupied, not paying attention to what is going on, not finishing sentences, and indulging in annoying double-checking. Think of the myriad symptoms of anxiety, and it is not difficult to see how a person experiencing these could get into minor misunderstandings with the rest of the family.

The two second-stage symptoms, loss of the capacity for emotional control and loss of the ability to motivate the self, are very likely to cause major disputes. People experiencing stage-two symptoms are irritable and easily upset; they lose their temper and throw things, and then just as quickly settle down. It is often the unpredictability associated with the loss of temper that most bothers friends and relatives. Loved ones may have to decide to keep the overstressed person at arms' length, not knowing what to say or what not to say, to avoid the explosions.

People demonstrating the other symptom of stage two, the loss of the ability to motivate themselves, are usually accused of being lazy. This accusation is particularly damaging when the overstressed person is the mother of a newborn infant. Women are deeply hurt by accusations of laziness—in contrast to men, who are hurt by the accusation of uselessness.

## Complex communication problems in stage three

The first symptom of stage-three breakdown is that sensory stimulation becomes disagreeable and the person begins to avoid interacting with others. This behavior may be mistaken for aloofness or arrogance and cause others to feel slighted and ignored. Avoidance of stimulation can also reduce the overstressed person's interest in sex. A sudden decrease in sexual interest may lead his or her sexual partner to suspect an affair. And when this suspicion is aired, arguments may start.

The second symptom is a loss of tolerance, a loss of the ability to not react to things previously put up with for years. This loss of tolerance might mean an overstressed boss could suddenly become fanatic about enforcing strict rules that had lapsed into nonobservance. Or this symptom might cause a sudden intolerance of personality differences between husband and wife. In my practice, I have often seen couples suffering from stress breakdown symptoms who are now complaining about the very personality differences that made each other so interesting years ago.

The third symptom of third-stage stress breakdown is the apparent change of personality and priorities caused by the brain's circuit breaker mechanisms shutting down the overloaded circuits. The communication problems which result from this changed pattern of response can be very complex.

For example, big problems, previously agreed on by a married couple as having first priority, may appear now to be trivialized or ignored by the over-stressed person. Furthermore, unimportant matters will be attended to as usual. When both husband and wife are suffering from third-stage stress break-down, it becomes virtually impossible to discuss their major problems, as they both switch off if any attempt is made to raise important issues.

In normal patterns of communication, it is often what we avoid saying that contains the real message. For example, when a relative is asking after various members of the family, the one who isn't mentioned may be the one out of favor. Thus failing to mention something important when we are expected to discuss it, might represent an important communication in itself. And not mentioning important issues is a symptom of stress breakdown.

English is a tonal language. We can easily alter the whole meaning of a sentence by changing the emphasis on certain words. For example, these seemingly identical sentences have different meanings:

Would **you** help me?
Would you **help** me?
Would you help **me?**
**Would** you help me?

Furthermore, we may use excessive emphasis on emotive words to convey the opposite meaning to what we seem to be saying. For example, the sarcastic comment: "Isn't he **clever**?" really isn't praise at all. Thus meaningful pauses, facial expressions and tone, are very important in conveying meaning in spoken language. Under conditions of stress breakdown, the ability to respond to tonal communication and to communicate by significant restraint, is seriously impaired.

## I was only joking!

Comedy depends on the ability of the listener to respond to the inconsistency and the inappropriateness of the subject matter. As these capacities are lost in severe stress breakdown, the person loses his or her sense of humor. Conversely, the return of a good sense of humor is a reliable sign of recovery from severe stress breakdown.

# CHAPTER NINE
## Prevention of Marriage Breakdown Under Stress

The last two chapters have described a number of differences between men and women, and also possible sources of conflict within relationships. Even under ordinary circumstances these differences may be enough to cause significant tensions between husband and wife. Under stressful conditions they can cause irretrievable family breakdown. Stress reactions enhance the destructiveness of these sources of conflict in three main ways:

1. The differences themselves can be a source of stress, contributing to the total load on the nervous system's processing capacity, enough to tip the balance towards stress breakdown. A good example is the difference in negotiating style between men and women. A man nearly failing to cope with the stress of a hiring and firing job may be tipped into stress breakdown by having to come to a negotiated settlement through a series of discussions with his wife or some other woman important in his life. He finds it difficult to adapt to her seemingly confronting opening statements. In reality, as explained above, she is not challenging him at all, merely starting the negotiations.

2. Stress reactions can bring altered behavior which may magnify differences that already exist. An example would be the second symptom of stage

three: the sudden loss of tolerance for things we have previously put up with. When people lose the capacity to tolerate personality traits they usually see as harmless eccentricities, a wedge of non-acceptance is driven between them, widening the emotional distance.

3. Stress reactions can interfere with adaptive mechanisms which normally bridge differences between people in close relationships. For example, sexual intimacy between two people who have loved each other for many years can often bridge a gap when words seem only to bring conflict. However, the stage-three symptom of avoidance of sensory stimulation can so interfere with a couple's normal sex life that the honest tenderness of sexual intimacy is unavailable to soothe hurt feelings.

## First aid to stressed marriages

If you think your own marriage could be under threat from stress breakdown, I offer you the following advice:

- Consider the diagnosis. If the problem is stress breakdown, and you are both trying to sort your problems out with psychotherapy, forget your therapy until you are both rested and feeling well. You need rest, relief of stress and increased sleep, both of you.

- Don't make wrong assumptions, particularly about the meaning of a lack of interest in your sex life. It all comes back when stress breakdown symptoms are relieved.

130

- Begin adopting a lower-stress lifestyle straight-away, including strict rest for one day a week, and frequent breaks during your busy day. Get away from the telephone at the weekend.

- Don't do anything unusual or make any major decisions while you are under stress. You may not be able to plan things well because of stress breakdown. You are not likely to be able to make decisions about separation or divorce.

- Don't think divorce is necessarily the solution. While it promises some freedom and peace and quiet in bed for a change, divorce can lead to stressful loneliness. Statistics show that the chances of marriage number two breaking down are much the same as for the first marriage. This indicates that working to prevent breakdown of your current relationship is well worth the effort.

## We must respect the basic mystery

Love between husband and wife is a deep mystery, deepened further by biblical concepts of married love as reflecting the love of God towards human beings, and yet God is love itself. It seems that love, like the nature of God, is unknowable. Therefore we cannot know how to make someone fall in love, and we cannot improve or repair a love relation-ship. The best we can do in strained marriages is to remove any hindrances to the free expression of love between husband and wife.

Marriage counseling requires great sensitivity, and it must consist of more than simply outlining dis-agreements between husbands and wives. Because of biological and behavioral differences, men and women will have different versions of the same events taking place at home. A sensitive resolution of the issues driving them apart is going to require the active loving cooperation of both.

## Sharing your family histories

In my experience, the most useful thing a couple can do for their marriage is to try to understand the prejudices and fears that each has brought to the marriage from their family of origin. The best approach to this is to write down, together, both of your family trees in diagram form.

I would advise that you set aside two hours to do this, and begin with Mum and Dad. Write down your descriptions of their personalities, and how they make decisions. Then extend the family tree upwards to include mothers' and fathers' families of origin, noting down everything you know about them. Also any notes about yourself, and your own brothers and sisters.

A sample family tree is given opposite.

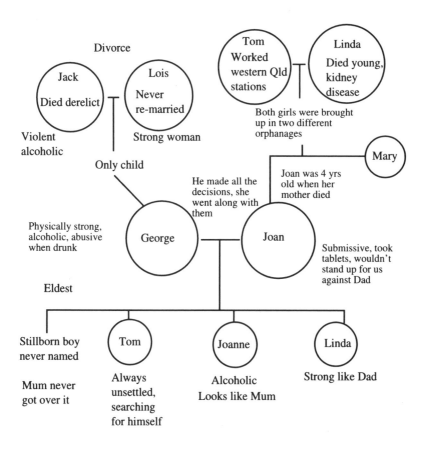

There is a wealth of information available from even the sketchy outline Tom has recorded so far about his own family tree. The first thing we note is that Tom's father and mother have very different personalities, and therefore Tom will have internalized both of these people, so that they become two different aspects of his self-control system. There are two sides to Tom, a strong abusive side he does not like because his father's behavior was unacceptable to him, and a submissive side he also does not like, corresponding to the submissive behavior of his mother, which disappointed him.

Immediately we know something about Tom's vulnerability related to these characteristics. He would have a tendency to dislike himself whenever he finds himself being critical of his children, as his father was, or lacking assertiveness like his mother.

Tom may also have internalized his father George's attitude to women. George's mother Lois was a very strong woman who controlled him, often reminding George what a terrible life she had led with George's father Jack. George has projected his fear of being smothered by a woman, plus his dependency, on his wife Joan. He's tried to deal with his own fears of rejection by controlling Joan's life totally, making sure she is dependent on him. For her part, Joan is a survivor, growing up in an institution, learning to conform to authority and agreeing with what other people say.

Tom will have developed some mixed feelings towards his mother. When Tom was born, Joan was afraid she'd lose this baby too. She tended to project some of the fears left over from losing her mother, onto the risk of losing Tom. So Joan tended to overprotect Tom when he was little. Tom resented his mother's attempt to smother him emotionally.

We also know from experience that the unconscious mind of a married man often confuses wife, mother and eldest daughter. In the same way a married woman's unconscious mind may confuse husband, father and eldest son. Tom is very likely to behave in such a way as to turn his wife into a carbon copy of his mother Joan without knowing he is doing it.

Because George dominated Joan, Tom would have identified more with George than Joan. Children usually model the behavior of the dominant parent; the ability to do this is built into us. It would be evolutionary suicide to model one's behavior on the seemingly ineffective parent. Therefore, although Tom knows how to be soft and diplomatic like his mother Joan, if he is in the middle of a crisis he will tend to adopt an abusive attitude like his father George.

There is much more an experienced therapist might infer about the pattern of prejudices and fears Tom has brought to his marriage. From his perspective, if he searches carefully, he will find within himself some remnant of all these people appearing in his family history, all having some influence on the way he relates to his wife and family.

## Understanding introjection

Up to the age of about 6 years, children normally internalize an accurate copy of the mannerisms and attitudes of both parents. This occurs at the same time as language and other skills are becoming automatic, and involves the same process. We don't have to think about the words we speak in our mother language. In the same way we automatically behave towards others and ourselves in exactly the same way our parents behaved towards us.

Thus the behavior of the people who care for us in early childhood is introjected or internalized to become the basic structure on which our own self-control system is based. If we are fortunate, our parents' behavior will be non-violent, predictable and fair. And we will grow up to be fair-minded and flexible in our attitudes towards ourselves and our loved ones. If our parents were critical and hard to please, we will be self-critical and exacting towards ourselves and others. A relationship between real people, our parents and us, has been introjected and is destined to become a relationship between parts of the mind.

It is important to realize that these internalized parents will remain part of our own functioning for a lifetime. Whether we approve of their behavior or not, even if we have vowed never to behave like them, we will surely do so, to the same extent we continue to speak English throughout life with the particular accent we developed in childhood. The internalized interactions between mother and father themselves will also stay part of us, to become the way the two basic parts of us, derived from mother and father, relate to each other in the mind.

For example, a man I know has a pattern of behavior which resembles mood swings. His father was very outgoing and optimistic, his mother was a quiet pessimist. When his father did or said something that offended his mother, she would withdraw and not speak for days. This man has a behavior pattern just the same. If in a jocular mood he does or says something he thinks may have offended someone, he will sulk for days, not speaking to anyone.

In explaining the process of introjection, I find very few people realize how permanent this is. Psychiatrists often use the term plasticity of the nervous system to describe the way the nervous system can be permanently shaped by early experience. Just as plasticine does not spring back into shape, the circuits programmed into the human brain by early childhood experience tend to remain, although later experiences may impose extra changes. However, the chances of changing the effects of early experiences diminish as the child grows older.

## Repeating unacceptable behavior

We cannot help acting like Mum or Dad. But what if their behavior was totally unacceptable? Does this mean we have a tendency to repeat their mistakes? Unfortunately yes. The sins of the parents may be "visited" on the children up to the third and fourth generations.

The reason this is relevant to marriage counseling in overstressed families is that the burning desire of a husband or wife not to repeat the mistakes of a parent can cause major stress within the marriage. Attempts to avoid situations that occurred in the family of origin may paradoxically result in their repetition. I have seen this happen many times. For example Alice, the daughter of an alcoholic father, is so distressed by her father's unpredictably nasty behavior while drunk, she vows and declares she will never allow any man to control her. Of the people who want to take her out, Henry is reliable and does exactly what she wants. He's in fact hiding lots of fears, and is grateful for Alice's strength, although he does feel smothered by her at times. They get married. Suddenly one day, Henry discovers that alcohol makes him feel normal and gives him a bit of confidence to come home and give Alice a good talking to. Alice's need to control a man who might control her has set up a control conflict situation. And she has married an alcoholic without knowing it.

## Doing what you say you're not doing

Over years of clinical practice I have seen many examples of people behaving just like the parent whose behavior was intolerable, and yet denying at the same time they were doing so. One woman, for example, claimed she always allowed her children to express themselves freely, because her parents had never let her talk about her fears. And yet it was obvious on seeing her interact with her children that they felt emotionally suppressed. She had unknowingly trained her own children never to tell her anything that would upset her. As a result, they felt as suppressed as she had felt as a child.

Parents who have vowed never to do something that they are in reality doing can cause a lot of stress in the family. It is very difficult for a child to know what to say to this parent under such conditions.

## Are we doomed to repeat our parents' mistakes?

We all tend to repeat our parents' mistakes, but we are not compelled to do so. We inherit tendencies, appetites, fears and prejudices, but we are responsible for our own behavior. An angry man from an angry family can learn to count ten before making a reply, and soften his response. A jealous woman from a jealous family can likewise learn to bite her lip instead of making a hurtful accusation.

However, the route to freedom from the errors of

our parents involves an open acknowledgment of these errors. A healing method called "Healing the Family Tree," where people apologize for their ancestors' mistakes, is very helpful in freeing people from a compulsion to repeat these errors.

## Problems passing down generations

My experience of recording family histories has taught me that when one generation does not adequately deal with a problem, the next generation is forced to do so. Divorce is a good example. Mum and Dad could not find a way to reconcile their differences and they split up. However, the children want to love both mother and father, and also want to believe in marriage. So they search for reasons in their own minds for why their parents broke up and try to forgive them both for their mistakes. They try to find the bridge between mother and father that their parents were unable or unwilling to try to find for themselves.

Another example is violence. I knew a man who refused to physically discipline his children. He told me his own father had been a very cruel man, and his father before him. This man told me he had his father's violence within him and, if he began beating his children, he might not be able to stop. When his children misbehaved, he was thrown into an inner turmoil and became anxious. He suffered a great deal because of his father's violence, yet because he himself was never violent to his children, they knew nothing of violence. They just knew their Dad was a soft touch. What had happened was that the violence had come down the family tree until an innocent person had suffered for it: in Christian terminology, until an innocent person had been crucified. The suffering of an innocent person had stopped the transmission of the sin.

## The family as a microcosm

In families under stress, inappropriate emotional reactions, intolerance and impaired communication will make it difficult to see clearly the points I have been making. But all these processes and more will be happening and affecting the quality of family life. The family is a microcosm, a miniature society, in which people play out major themes affecting society as a whole. Many families in recent years have been arguing about major issues such as feminism and homosexuality. Everything happening in the world will be reflected in families and argued about. In overstressed families, these imported frustrations can become quite disruptive.

An accurate assessment of what is really going on in the family, what has been imported from outside, and what contribution has come from the family heritage, requires a lot of training and skill. However, if a married couple without any training in this area were to sit down quietly and discuss their family histories without any preconceived ideas and without assigning blame, they might achieve a great deal of common understanding.

# CHAPTER TEN
## Post-Traumatic Stress Disorders

People who have survived stressful events or periods in their lives may never be able to forget what happened. They may have nightmares over and over of the same event. Sometimes a chance stimulus will remind them of the event and they may instantly react as if it were happening all over again. They may feel edgy a lot of the time, as though constantly on the lookout for danger. And sometimes they feel numb, alienated from people around them, able to share memories of the event only with others who were there at the time. We call this a post-traumatic stress disorder.

What causes it? It seems that the memory of a stressful event includes a memory of body feelings in just the same way that pleasant memories may be associated with smells or sounds. Recalling the event recalls the complex distressing feelings of stress breakdown which were experienced at the time. And because people don't like feeling anxious and distressed, they will avoid recalling the memory. So it sits there, half-forgotten, like an open wound that's never been closed or a bruise that's never healed.

Psychiatrists detect these painful memories during history-taking. We notice an emotional reaction when the patient mentions the event. A tear in the eye, a changed expression, a change in facial color, a tremble of the lip, a quaver in the voice. What is happening is that at that moment the patient is re-experiencing all over again a sample of the symptoms of stress breakdown endured at the time. The event might be some form of physical or sexual abuse in childhood, an act of brutality in war or the humiliation of being held hostage during an armed robbery. Any traumatic event that we might describe as outside normal human experience can produce a post-traumatic stress disorder.

However, very many people suffer post-traumatic stress symptoms from events which are unfortunately becoming part of everyday experience: being repeatedly bullied at school, being harassed out of jobs by bosses doing their workplace restructuring on the cheap, or being victimized for being a "whistleblower."

## False memory syndrome

In recent times, there has been considerable debate over memories of childhood abuse which have been recalled for the first time by a patient undergoing counseling or some form of hypnotic regression therapy. This debate is more than just of academic interest. I have seen cases where men have faced criminal charges, where the evidence appeared to be based on remembered fantasies rather than remembered events.

False memories have a quality of their own. Because they originate in dreams and wishful thinking, they are not limited by anatomical or logical constraints. Thus false memories of sexual abuse might be recalled without awareness of the physical differences in size between a grown man and a small child.

Adults returning to a childhood home may find the buildings and the surroundings are in reality much smaller than in their memories. They then realize they remembered these things as they would have appeared through the eyes of a child. By contrast, false memories from childhood are often recalled as though by a person of unlimited dimensions.

Many false memories are fragments of childhood dreams and fantasies, recalled in later life as though the events actually happened. Like the fantasies of origin, these false recollections are often logically impossible. And like dreams, recall is usually variable and inconsistent.

## When you try to forget and you cannot

In contrast to the difficulties in remembering false memories, real memories of emotionally traumatic events are very hard to forget. A man came to see me for help to get rid of a sequence of memories that plagued him night after night. He had been a soldier in Vietnam, riding on the front of an armoured personnel carrier (APC) when the APC traveling in front ran over a land mine. The soldiers riding at the rear of the APC in full view had their legs blown off by the explosion. He felt emotionally paralyzed, helpless, and very much afraid.

Very many years later, in spite of having made his peace with Vietnamese people, forgiven everybody he could think of and dealt with the memories as best he knew how, this man would wake in the middle of the night, experiencing the emotions he felt at the time of this incident. He would lie awake, feeling helpless, distressed and very much afraid, and he assumed he had just been dreaming about the event, although he could not remember the dream.

I was unable to be of much help to this man, but I referred him to a doctor who was using a technique called EMDR (Eye Movement Desensitization Reprocessing). In this technique, the person recalls the traumatic memory while moving their eyes to and fro, in a simulation of eye movements occurring naturally in dreaming or Rapid Eye Movement (REM) sleep. After a few sessions the man was healed of the recurring emotional flashbacks.

Past traumatic events and their associated details may be remembered in distressing clarity for a lifetime. A woman I know remembers being made to stand in a waste paper basket for being a dunce when she was in grade one at school. She says she will never forget it. Holocaust survivors say they will never forget the faces of their tormentors.

This inability to forget real trauma is the main reason that experienced therapists are suspicious of memories recalled for the first time under therapy. Damaged people do not have difficulty recalling traumatic events, they have difficulty forgetting them. I accept that people may repress memories of a guilty past, and that it is possible an unscrupulous adult might convince a little girl she had initiated a sexual act, and that little girl might repress memories of her guilty secret. However, in my experience children do remember, but are too ashamed to mention it. I think memories recalled for the first time under therapy are unlikely to relate to actual trauma, but probably represent memories of day-dreams, fears, nightmares and scenes from films and television.

## Treatment for post-traumatic stress symptoms

I do not live or work in a war zone. I was reflecting recently how little violence I have seen in the sub-urb I live in. In thirty years I have never witnessed a fist fight in the street. My area is a relatively peace-ful place to live.

Likewise the cases of post-traumatic stress disor-der I have had to treat are not usually related to civil war, terrorism or earthquakes. They are more likely to involve a different form of violence. For example, I have treated more cases of police officers dam-aged by the persecution of bureaucracy than in shoot-outs with desperate criminals. I have seen more school teachers harassed by their own school principals than by adolescent gangs. I have seen many sensitive people brutalized by psychiatric evaluation and labeling, for whom ongoing psychi-atric treatment had to include treatment for symp-toms directly caused by the violence of labeling and disrespect. And in the last few years I have had referred to me an increasing number of people who have broken down emotionally from being harassed at their place of employment.

In recent times, big words like economic rational-ism have been telling us it is good to be lean and mean. It seems that the days of generous early retirement packages are over. Job restructuring now seems to begin with importing an expert in "downsizing." This person or organization then uses sophisticated tactics to bully and harass vulnerable people in the workforce into resigning, taking enforced retirement, or being superannuated out on medical grounds.

Bullying—the victimization of the weak by the strong—is sadly becoming an administrative strategy.

## The effects of victimization

Our society often tries to blame the victim for the harassment. We send the victims of school bullies off for counseling, we tell the battered wives it is their own fault for staying with their abusive husbands. We describe whistleblowers as having personality disorders and accuse them of being misfits in society.

I usually find the first and most important part of treating victims of bullying is to reassure them they did not cause their own victimization. The bullied child needs to be reassured, "You are not to blame," because people will try to make excuses for the bullying. "Look, that kid's strange, nobody likes him. He pulls his pants up too high, and he parts his hair in the middle. It is no wonder the other kids pick on him." The list of annoying characteristics which exonerate the bullies is very long indeed. Bullies will pick on you if you are black, white, Chinese, Caucasian, small, tall, fat, thin, you wear glasses, you have got pimples, you haven't got pimples, your clothes are shabby, your clothes are neat, you are dumb, or you are smart. The truth is, bullies pick on you if they think you will not strike back.

The most damaging effect of victimization is that the victims tend to do the same to themselves. They blame themselves for the bullying, accusing themselves of cowardice, of being weak and defective because they feel hurt by the criticisms of their tormentors. So the first thing to do is to stop the victims from blaming themselves.

## Steps in treatment of post-traumatic stress disorders

**The first step** is to give the patient with a post-traumatic stress disorder the status of a damaged person. Thus the abused child is someone who was abused, not a bad person. The child bullied at school is someone who was victimized, not a coward. The worker harassed out of his job is an injured worker, eligible for workers' compensation.

**The second step** is to examine the memories of the traumatic events, and try to fit them into some meaningful framework. If the victim can see why the bully acted the way he did, the events begin to make sense. At this stage there is no thought whatsoever of making excuses for the bullying behavior, just simply to make sense of it. A senior lecturer, forced into giving tutorials in a subject he had never been trained for, by superiors intending to force him to resign, felt relieved when a friend overheard some of these people bragging about their dirty tricks campaign.

This part of the therapy for post-traumatic stress disorder can be challenging. A psychiatric nurse had never recovered from the trauma of a patient trying

147

to strangle her. She saw in this man's eyes sheer hatred, palpable evil. A major problem in her rehabilitation was that her psychiatric training had no explanation for evil—representing malice as either ignorance or mental illness, but she knew the malevolence she saw in his eyes was neither of those.

**The third step** in the treatment of post-traumatic stress disorders is to reclaim the ground that has been lost. The person returns to the place, to the role, or to the expectations that existed before the trauma. The bank clerk who has been robbed and held hostage prepares to return to the job. The woman who was sexually abused by her stepfather accepts his apology. In this third step, the skills of the therapist are strongly tested. The traumatized person does not want to return to the place where it all happened, and yet knows that unless he does he will always be a victim.

Sometimes techniques using visual imagery, where the person returns to the traumatic scene in imagination, can be useful here. I personally do not use hypnosis or EMDR, but other therapists find these techniques helpful. It is important not to try to use such techniques to force a cure on the person with post-traumatic stress disorder. In my experience a patient will not be healed until the traumatic experience makes sense in some way. There is no substitute for the second step.

### Why people may not get better for many years

The most important fact about people with post-traumatic stress disorders is that the symptoms don't just go away with the passage of time. Some therapists even hold the view that people can be permanently damaged by severe emotional stress. I don't agree; there is usually some psychological process operating to explain long-lasting disability.

For example, a woman was forcibly taken to a mental hospital after her husband had manipulated a psychiatrist into taking illegal action against her. Although the hospital found she was perfectly normal, the husband later made successful use of the fact that she had once been certified to hospital to damage her credibility in the Family Court. Years later, she is still experiencing symptoms of post-traumatic stress disorder, because her ex-husband insists the children accept his story that their mother was mentally ill. The reason she is still suffering from post-traumatic symptoms is that she is still being victimized by the same lie.

## The fruits of school bullying

Negative emotions like shame and fear are excellent reinforcers of learning. I wonder how many people who saw the Hitchcock movie *Psycho* only once, many years ago, are still a little anxious about closing their eyes in the shower. The experience of being a bully, a victim, or a bystander and keeping silent, are all potent reinforcers of learning. But what is being learned by our children in the schools that turn a blind eye to bullying?

The bullies learn how to intimidate people successfully. Many perfect these skills enough to earn them prison terms later on. Other school bullies who stay out of jail use their skills bullying wives and workmates. The bystanders learn not to see victimization going on around them, for fear of becoming victims themselves. They grow up to become the silent majority who allow bullies to take over governments and institutions.

What do the victims learn? Some victims play truant, refuse to go to school, and learn that authority is powerless when you choose not to cooperate with it. Some bullied children experience the symptoms of stage-three stress breakdown. Suddenly they refuse to tolerate their situation, and react in a way that is totally out of character. Suddenly they may lash out with a weapon, they may snap and do something out of control. In schools that turn a blind eye to bullying, an out-of-control reaction by a victimized child may be the first indication of anything wrong. Therefore the victim may be labeled as the troublemaker, or as having some psychiatric problem.

Sometimes, unpredictable violence from a victimized person stops the bullying. The others become afraid of what this person might do if put under stress again. In this case, what is the lesson learned? Overreact, make trouble, look after number one. Don't allow anyone to control you.

The children of unpredictably violent alcoholic fathers provide us with a good example of victims on a steep learning curve. These people often grow up with a need to be in control of whatever is happening.

# CHAPTER ELEVEN
## When Stress Makes Us Physically Ill

We all know that too much psychological stress can make us physically ill. This chapter will try to explain how.

### Anxiety

Let us look first at the symptom of free-floating anxiety, the first sign we are breaking down under stress. It is a vague, urgent feeling of unease or dread, and is accompanied by a whole range of body symptoms caused by changes in body function in preparation for fight or flight.

The symptom of anxiety itself is distressing enough for some people to think they might be ill. Particularly if there is another symptom as well, for example, the symptom of *hypoglycemia* or low blood glucose. Here the body responds with an anxiety reaction to a drop in blood glucose that itself interferes with brain function. The person is nervy, confused, and cannot think straight.

Some occupations repeatedly make people anxious throughout a normal working day, for instance, the electronic media. People working in radio and television, who make important split-second decisions all day every day, may often experience free-floating anxiety. This possibility may be greatly enhanced by the habit of drinking endless cups of strong coffee. Repeated changes in blood flow and the activity of internal organs associated with preparation for fight or flight, may over a period of time produce illness. Patterns of these illnesses vary greatly, and are highly individual. For example, I experience symptoms caused by spasm of the lower esophagus whenever I have to be the peacemaker in situations of conflict. And when I feel I would like to run away, my legs ache.

One very common symptom occurring in jobs or lifestyles where people have to react quickly to the unexpected, is tension headache. Just observe a person who is preparing to react to the unexpected. The head is held rigidly upright, neck and upper shoulders tight. These muscles cannot relax, and so become stiff and very sore. I remember a young man, working in a community radio station, who had a chronic headache. It was his job to respond immediately to information on the Teletext and instantly break into normal programs with radio news flashes. When he was given different work to do, he lost his chronic headache.

## Parasympathetic reaction

When we are constantly on edge, experiencing first-stage stress breakdown symptoms repeatedly, the body has to adapt to being frequently put on alert. When the body is prepared for fight or flight, and blood flow diverted away from non-essential functions, a range of body functions necessary for good housekeeping are not being done. As a reaction to this, the nerve network that opposes fight or flight reactions is stimulated. This network, the parasympathetic nervous system, is usually active during rest and recuperation. The body finds it necessary to have to oppose the effects of adrenalin and noradrenaline that are regularly being released with frequent anxiety reactions. The battle between the two systems can lead to irregular contractions in many hollow organs in the body, with spasm and associated pain as a result. Irritable bowel symptoms, frequency of urination and hunger pains are common examples.

## Overeating

While we may experience a whole range of symptoms associated with the warning signal of anxiety, we usually damage our health more by trying to avoid anxiety than we do by experiencing anxiety.

Overeating and snacking would probably be the most common activity which we use to reduce anxiety. This mechanism to reduce anxiety has been thoroughly incorporated into the behavioral patterns of our culture. For example, it is common practice to invite someone to dinner to soften the blow from the bad news we have to convey. Prudent people will wait until the victim is well fed before revealing the worst. Caring therapists or counselors will often offer their anxious clients a cup of tea or coffee.

However pleasant it is to make ourselves feel better by rewarding snacks and sweets, eating when we are not hungry provides the body with far more fuel than it needs, and at inappropriate times. The result is often obesity and all the health problems associated with being overweight.

153

## Alcohol

Human beings have been using and abusing alcohol to handle anxiety symptoms since at least the time of the ancient Egyptians. However, the alcohol content of beer in those days was fairly low because ancient brewers didn't know about sterilization, and they hadn't invented distillation to produce pure alcohol. For the last 300 years, human beings have been increasingly poisoning themselves with high alcohol drinks. Alcohol was our first sedative drug, and it is still the most abused sedative, being freely available without a doctor's prescription. Diseases caused by drinking alcohol include brain damage, stomach disorders, liver damage, alcoholic heart disease, pancreatitis, and disease of the peripheral nerves.

## Cigarette smoking

During World War II, prisoner-of-war aid packages always contained cigarettes, and many doctors advised their patients to take up cigarette smoking to reduce anxiety. Nicotine is an unusual drug. In small doses it appears to function as a stimulant, in high doses it has a sedative action. People who smoke to reduce anxiety symptoms are usually smoking heavily. We now know, of course, how dangerous cigarette smoking is, particularly in its effect on arteries, in causing heart attacks and strokes.

## Complex patterns of preparedness—the "as if" syndromes

Most of what is happening in our bodies at the moment is not under conscious control. We are largely unaware of the unconscious mind making decisions, responding to problems, nourishing, repairing, supporting and preparing us for conscious mental activity. There are a number of stress-related illnesses caused by the unconscious mind preparing the body for action. I call these the "as if" syndromes.

### "As if" I am fighting for my life

There was an interesting article in a medical journal a few years ago about the use of onions and garlic to reduce the risk of thrombosis—that is, clotting of blood within veins and arteries. It was based on an old French veterinary remedy for thrombosis in horses, and it sparked off some witty letters to the editor about this proposed method of preventing heart attacks. An experiment was described where medical students going in to examinations had their blood tested for its clotting ability, with or without a meal of onions. The researchers purported to show that the students without prior onions showed an increased tendency for the blood to clot, as a result of the stress of the examinations.

What interested me more than the onions or their effects on interpersonal relationships was that the blood of healthy young people should be more ready to clot when they go "to do battle" with the examiners. I have heard that people in "hiring and firing" jobs have a higher risk of heart attack. (Heart attacks are usually caused by a clot of blood blocking up the coronary artery to the heart—coronary thrombosis.) It is "as if" the person going out to face some conflict has his body made ready to respond to a possible loss of blood. It is said that soldiers sustaining severe wounds in battle often don't bleed much at all, whereas if a person sustains a severe unexpected wound, as in the case of a butcher severing a femoral artery while "boning" the ribs of a carcass, there is a real risk of dying immediately from loss of blood. Clearly, readiness for conflict can minimize blood loss.

It is "as if" the body tones up the blood vessels so they are all ready to shut down the moment they are severed, and the blood made ready to clot at a moment's notice. Unfortunately, if the battle involves a politician under attack from his opponents, having to defend himself against a barrage of criticism, then the toned up blood vessels, and quick-clotting blood would be of no good use to him at all. Instead, the increased tone of the blood vessels and the extra clotting ability might cause a clot to form in a vein or artery. I remember that the late President Richard Nixon suffered from thrombosis of his leg veins, when he was in a beleaguered state prior to his resignation.

## "As if" I am hanging on by the skin of my teeth

There are many patterns of preparedness characterized by chronic contraction of specific muscle groups. A common pattern is seen in the person who is expecting the worst and has his teeth clenched and head held rigidly in anticipation. This may cause severe pain in the temporo-mandibular joint in front of the ear, as well as headaches and neck pain. In general, I find that people who are always psychologically bracing themselves for disaster tend to suffer stiffness and pain of the extensor muscles of the body. These include not only the muscles at the back of the neck, but those of the shoulders and the lower back, as well.

### "As if" I am starving to death

Diabetes mellitus, or "sugar diabetes," used to be considered a psychosomatic disorder, particularly when it was discovered that the extra cortisol released by the adrenal cortex under conditions of stress tends to increase the body's blood glucose level, and produce symptoms similar to diabetes.

However, there is now no real need to think of diabetes mellitus as a psychosomatic disorder (it does not avail us much), because the treatment of diabetes is by insulin injections and diet, or diet and pills, or diet alone. However, I have been surprised at the number of diabetic patients who have in their history a significant cause of deep insecurity, an insecurity so profound that they may have feared, at least unconsciously, starving to death.

In diabetes mellitus, the body behaves "as if" it only has fat from the body stores to live on, "as if" it is starving to death. The body seems to ignore food coming in to the stomach, with regard to secreting suitable quantities of insulin at least, and occupies itself with breaking down stores of body fat. The result is a combination of excess acid in the blood from breaking down fat, plus an inability to metabolize carbohydrates, with excess glucose flowing out in the urine.

Let me say, however, that while this theory is an interesting one, and attention should be paid to deeply held fears of abandonment and starvation, the correct treatment of diabetes mellitus is by the medically proven methods of diet, hypoglycemic drugs, and insulin.

## "Organ language"

When we come to consider other ways in which symbolism might produce body symptoms, we need to consider *organ language*. People sometimes express their emotions and feelings by using words appropriate to the function of organs in the body. When I was a resident medical officer, I saw an adolescent girl in the hospital casualty department complaining of painful red areas on the sides of the neck. This girl was very tense and irritable. She said, "My mother is a pain in the neck! Whatever I do is wrong, I cannot win, and I am sick of it!" We might say that this girl was literally "hot under the collar."

Other people complain that someone "makes me sick in the stomach!"—thereby giving some clue as to the cause of symptoms of nausea and diarrhea.

Some people adopt a "stiff-necked" approach to criticism by refusing to respond to it, holding their heads up with pride and perhaps suffering from neck pain.

Another common example of organ language is "globus hystericus": the development of the "feeling" of a lump in the throat, which does not in any way interfere with the person's ability to swallow. (We must of course always exclude organic causes first, before diagnosing this symptom as psychosomatic.) It has been, in my experience anyway, associated with a feeling of "I am not going to swallow that!"—meaning of course, "I am not going to naively accept what you are trying to ram down my throat!"

I remember a patient who developed this symptom when her ex-husband, at the last minute in a property settlement court case following their divorce, suddenly tried to force her to accept terms of settlement that would be humiliating to her. She actually said to me, "I wasn't going to swallow that rubbish!"

## Health problems in stage-two stress breakdown

Stage-two stress breakdown is a state of fatigue, of exhaustion of the nervous system's inhibitory reserves. Often a lack of sufficient sleep has been a factor, along with excess stress. The body may have been deprived of sufficient opportunity for repair, which it usually attends to during sleep. Therefore in stage-two stress breakdown we become vulnerable to two groups of illnesses:

Illness related to depletion of neurotransmitters
Illnesses related to interrupted repair

Amongst the depletion illnesses I would include those where the body does not seem to be able to come up with enough adrenalin and noradrenaline in response to a body challenge. Asthma, acute hay fever, urticaria and migraine are good examples.

The illnesses related to interrupted repair would include fibrositis and various types of myalgia (muscle pain and stiffness). They also include illnesses caused by bacteria, viruses or parasites which are normally present in the body. These organisms have

159

been allowed to get out of control because the body's energy reserves have been run down, and there has not been sufficient deep sleep to activate the white blood cells whose job it is to destroy them. These illnesses would include herpes virus infections, aphthous ulcers inside the mouth, lobar pneumonia, crops of boils and pimples, tonsillitis and urinary tract infections.

It is essential for people suffering from stage-two symptoms to pay attention to reducing the bacterial population on their skin and mucous membranes. Therefore, take showers rather than baths, and shower twice a day, using a clean dry towel each time. Drink extra clean water to flush out the urinary tract. Clean your teeth more regularly. Avoid fermented foods.

I have mentioned before that the unconscious mind has a range of responses which it will activate in certain circumstances. A common response in people who ignore their body's warning signals is that when the overstressed person will not rest, the body will trigger an illness which forces them to do so. A good example of this is the "weekend" migraine which prevents an overtired person from doing anything else on the weekend other than resting in bed, nursing a splitting headache.

## Body symptoms in stage-three breakdown

In stage-three stress breakdown overloaded circuits shut down. These overloaded circuits may be associated with a body part or body organ and, when the circuit shuts down, the function of this body part or organ can be temporarily impaired. The impairment will always be a reduction in function. For example:

| | |
|---|---|
| Seeing clearly | is associated with the eye |
| Doing something | is associated with the hand |
| Hearing something | is associated with the ear |
| Standing up for yourself | is associated with the lower back |
| Not running away | is associated with the legs |

Stress involving seeing something you don't want to see can cause impairment of vision. For example, a little girl became temporarily blind because she didn't want to see her mother having an affair with another man. It wasn't deliberate, but we can easily see the connection between the loss of function and the type of stress. We call these symptoms *conversion symptoms* because the stress has been converted into a symptom of absence of function. Where the function is merely impaired, we don't seem to have a name for the process, but we know what is causing it: the circuit breaker mechanisms which operate in stage-three stress breakdown.

It is relatively straightforward to see the connections between not wanting to see or hear, and impaired eye and ear function. It is often more difficult to see connections between emotional states and organ systems, although the organ language I mentioned previously can give us a clue.

Take for example, all those reflexes concerned with feeding oneself. We know from experience how easily changed these reflexes are. If you are used to eating your midday meal at 12 noon, your tummy will start to rumble then if it is not fed.

161

Change your schedule to a 2 pm meal and fairly soon it will not rumble at 12 noon, but at 2 pm.

I know from years of clinical experience that reflexes concerned with feeding oneself are associated with concepts of dependence and independence. If you are independent you can feed yourself. If you are dependent on someone, you expect to have to be fed by that person. I have been surprised over the years at how many people suffering from peptic ulcers have some conflict about their relative dependence or independence on a business partner. I often notice how the language of business and marketing is associated with feeding. For example, business people might be described as hungry for business or looking for a bigger slice of the cake.

Likewise, concepts of individual assertiveness, of being able to hold on in spite of people wanting you to let go, seem to be associated with the function of bladder and bowel sphincters. We all know rigid people who obstruct progress and will not let things pass. A lot of them have problems with hemorrhoids and anal fissures.

My aim in this chapter has been to demonstrate that it is not difficult to work out why people may become ill under stressful circumstances. With a little imagination, you will be able to discover all sorts of connections between patterns of stress and patterns of illness and, I hope, will develop creative approaches to prevention.

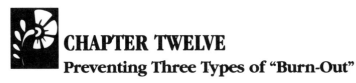

# CHAPTER TWELVE
## Preventing Three Types of "Burn-Out"

Over the years I have been asked for specific advice on the prevention of stress breakdown in various situations and occupations. In this final chapter I thought I might say something about preventing stress breakdown or "burn-out" in three high risk groups.

There are three burn-out situations in particular I would like to discuss:

- High performance burn-out of people in the public eye.

- Mothers of young children.

- Ministry burn-out. Here, I am referring generally to professional people whose job requires them to minister in some way to others. These include clergy and their wives, doctors, therapists of all sorts, counselors, social workers, psychologists, teachers and personnel support staff.

In the prevention of stress breakdown or burn-out generally, there are three basic essentials:

1. Whenever you experience free-floating anxiety you must see this as a warning signal and immediately evaluate what you are doing. Never ignore the warning.

2.  Should you demonstrate either of the two symptoms of stage two (loss of the capacity for emotional control, and loss of the ability to force yourself to keep going) you must put yourself to bed and replenish your neurotransmitter stores. You need to eat properly and rest. If you don't, you may become ill and your body (much smarter than you think), will force you to rest. Or else your nervous system will begin to malfunction with third-stage stress breakdown symptoms and everything will get out of control.

3.  You need at least one day off per week, to recuperate, to top up your energy reserves; doing nothing, just being. You may not expect I should have to make a point of this to clergy, but in fact clergy in all denominations often do not have a day off. They work when others rest, on their designated Sabbath. Many are supposed to have Mondays off, but their churches often schedule meetings for Mondays, and the general public usually don't know that the priest is not supposed to be available on Monday.

## High performance burn-out

As well as the above advice, people in high performance jobs or situations have a specific need to address the area of personal responsibility. Athletes, entertainers, teachers and politicians are always in danger of taking on too much responsibility and burning out under the load. I have often had to remind people in high performance jobs that they themselves are not the prime movers of their success. Although people will tell you that you and you alone achieved the successes for which you are so much admired, don't believe them. Our success came because we had an idea that other people wanted to hear, we had a plan they wanted to cooperate with, we had a dream they wanted to share.

All success is the outcome of cooperation in some way. Otherwise many of the great ideas would end up just like the drawings in Leonardo da Vinci's notebooks. The man was a genius, but he didn't make a submarine or a helicopter or a differential drive system. There were no engineering shops and foundries to make the right alloys. He didn't have enough knowledgeable people to cooperate with.

In my experience it is absolutely essential for people in high performance situations to live one day at a time, to live a twelve step lifestyle originating in the Twelve Steps of Alcoholics Anonymous. When people heap praise on you, don't believe it. If you are fooled into thinking you are doing it all, you will soon be frightened of the prospect of having to keep it up. Instead, say the Lord's Prayer every day, asking only for what you need that day, your instructions for the day, and the strength to carry it out.

## The mothers of young children

Women, you are in a unique position. When each of your babies was born and you met eye to eye for the first time, something happened. You fell in love, and that love affair never stops. You have a special relationship with each of your children, so special that for the rest of your life you will be part of each child's successes and failures and fears. No child will consider a venture complete unless Mum has heard about it or given approval. You will experience a lot of stress as a direct result of being so special:

- Your children will not happily accept being cared for by anyone else. It will be difficult for you to delegate responsibility for sick and frightened children.

- Our society will try to blame your children's personal problems and low self-esteem on your parenting.

My advice is that you put some effort into preventing stress breakdown. You should remember the wisdom of the Chinese people in insisting that the mother of a newborn baby do nothing at all for one month except breastfeed her baby and bathe herself. You should insist on that without feeling guilty. No cooking meals, no washing. You can eat, read, nurse your baby, think, watch TV, and have a well-earned rest. In doing so, you will replenish some of the energy reserves you invested in the previous nine months.

You should realize you have a right to ask for your partner's support. Ask for it, lean on him, and praise him. He wants to be useful, he wants to be supportive. When you have young children, you need all the support you can get.

In bringing up your children, you will have to make a variety of decisions for which you have no training or experience. I suggest you remember the proverb, "The fear of the Lord is the getting of wisdom." This means that in any new situation, if your attitude towards all concerned is one of respect, and you regard nothing in God's creation as second-rate, you will not make many big mistakes.

## Ministry burn-out

For years I have often wondered exactly what happens during psychotherapy sessions. Sometimes, feeling totally drained, I ask myself what I was doing during that time. Erecting pictures in my mind corresponding to what my patient was telling me, piecing them together, trying out little scenarios of what might work and what might apply. Sometimes the depletion of energy at the end of a session is extreme, and I may find later that this person has been concealing the truth.

Most people I know whose job involves ministering to others, share the same experience of being depleted by the process. It is as though we have a certain amount of caring to give out. In the gospels Jesus is reported to have noticed power going out of him when a woman, seeking healing, touched the hem of his garment.

Whatever is being depleted is replenished through rest and sleep. I have also found that some people suffering serious ministry burn-out may require small doses of antidepressant drugs to help the body restore the normal neurotransmitter levels.

My specific advice to clergy and all those involved in ministering to others is to take care not to run down your energy reserves. You must take holidays, and you need extra sleep. A short nap in the afternoon might prepare you for the evening counseling session. Remember Jesus himself had to get away on his own for a break from time to time. Don't attempt crash diets unless you are on holiday. And remember the parable of the foolish bridesmaids who didn't take reserves of oil, and their lamps burned out.

# BIBLIOGRAPHY

Archibald, H. C. & Tuddenham, R.D. "Persistent stress reaction following combat: a twenty-year follow up." *Archives of General Psychiatry,* vol. 12, 1965, pp. 475–81.

Boman, B. "The Vietnam veteran ten years on." *Australian and New Zealand Journal of Psychiatry,* vol. 16, 1982, pp. 107–27.

*DSM-III: Diagnostic and Statistical Manual of Mental Disorders.* 3rd ed. American Psychiatric Association, 1980.

Gil, D. "Physical Abuse of Children: findings and implications of a nationwide survey." *Paediatrics,* vol. 44, 1969, pp. 857–64.

Gitlow, S. "Sedativism and public trust," in "Alcoholism and Sedativism" audio cassette. *Audio-Digest Family Practice,* vol. 28, no. 42, 10 Nov., 1980.

Gray, J. A. (ed.) *Pavlov's Typology.* Pergamon Press, London, 1964.

Hora, T. *Existential Metapsychiatry.* Seabury Press, New York, 1977.

Luria, A. R. *The Working Brain.* Penguin Books, London.

Meares, A. *Life Without Stress*. Penguin Books, Melbourne, 1991.

O'Connor N. (ed.) *Present-day Russian Psychology,* Pergamon Press, London.

Pavlov, I. P. *Lectures on Conditioned Reflexes,* vols 1 & 2, trans. W. H. H. Gantt. International Publishers, New York. 1941.

Sargant, W. *"Battle for the Mind."* Heinemann, London, 1957.

Seneca. *"Letters From a Stoic."* Selected and translated by Robin Campbell. Penguin, 1969, pp. 197–8.

Schlesinger, L. B. & Revitch, E. "Stress, violence and crime," in *Handbook on Stress and Anxiety,* eds Kutash, Schlesinger et al. Jossey-Bass, 1981, p. 176.

Sheen, F. J. *Life is Worth Living,* Peter Davies Ltd, London.

Vitz, P. C. *Psychology as Religion.* Lion Publishing, England, 1979.

Walter, E. G. *The Living Brain.* Duckworth, London, 1953.

Wharton, L. H. "The Great Stoned Age." *Audio-Digest,* vol. 12, no. 21, 7 Nov. 1983.

Wilkie, W. *Understanding Psychiatry,* Hill of Content Publishing, Melbourne, 1987.

Wilkie, W. *The Doctor Bill Series—Radio Scripts,* W. C. and S. M. Wilkie Publishing, Brisbane, 1989.

# INDEX